D0793254

Art Center College of Design
Library
1700 Lida Street
Pasadena, Calif. 91103

ART CENTER COLLEGE OF DESIGN

3 3220 00208 7281

TRACING FILE
for Interior and Architectural Rendering

ART CENTER COLLEGE OF DESIGN LIBRARY
1700 LIDA STREET
PASADENA, CALIFORNIA 91103

Book Design by Gregory B. Madsen

TRACING FILE
for Interior and Architectural Rendering

Richard M. McGarry

720.284
M145
1988

VNR VAN NOSTRAND REINHOLD
New York

ACKNOWLEDGMENTS

Several people made significant contributions to the creation of this book. Wendy Lochner, my editor at Van Nostrand Reinhold, patiently guided and refined the book from concept through publication; and Greg Madsen, an associate at Richard M. McGarry Inc., created an excellent book design and composed the mechanicals for final print production. Lou and Steve Litzman, the father-and-son team at Photo Arts of Miami, did all the camera work in preparing the drawings for publication.

I would also like to thank several fellow artists and designers who have helped me develop my talent over the years: John Adams, Juan Corbella, Bill Hinnant, Ann Irvine, Martin Kanigsberg, Paul Kenson, and Rick MacDonald. Likewise, I am grateful to my clients, whose discerning critiques and frantic deadlines challenge me to continuously improve my work.

And a special thanks to Stephen Nevitt. His encouragement and support made this book possible.

Copyright © 1988 by Richard M. McGarry
Library of Congress Catalog Card Number 88-10235
ISBN 0-442-20530-9

All rights reserved. Interior designers, architects, design students, and graphic artists may trace or otherwise manually manipulate any images contained herein, but the book may not be mechanically or electronically reproduced as a whole or in substantial part.

Printed in the United States of America

Van Nostrand Reinhold
115 Fifth Avenue
New York, New York 10003

Van Nostrand Reinhold (International) Limited
11 New Fetter Lane
London EC4P 4EE, England

Van Nostrand Reinhold
480 La Trobe Street
Melbourne, Victoria 3000, Australia

Macmillan of Canada
Division of Canada Publishing Corporation
164 Commander Boulevard
Agincourt, Ontario M1S 3C7, Canada

16 15 14 13 12 11 10 9 8 7 6 5 4 3 2 1

Library of Congress Cataloging in Publication Data

McGarry, Richard M., 1948–
  Tracing file for interior and architectural rendering / Richard M. McGarry.
    p.   cm.
  Includes index.
  ISBN 0-442-20530-9 (pbk.)
  1. Interior decoration rendering.   2. Architectural rendering.   I. Title.
NK2113.5.M38   1988
720′.28′4—dc19   88-10235
                                                            CIP

PREVIOUS PAGE

The clusters of club chairs that comprise the bottom half of this cocktail lounge concept sketch would probably be too repetitive to hold a viewer's attention for long without the addition of customers to break up the chair pattern. Foreground luggage and airplanes seen through the glass in the distance help to tell the story that this is an airport lounge. PROJECT: Proposed Dobb's Airport Lounge, Miami International Airport; DESIGNER: Barry K. Slack, Robison & Associates, Inc., Interior Architecture.

CONTENTS

We may, without
offending any laws of
good taste, require of
an architect, as we do of a
novelist, that he should
be not only correct,
but entertaining.
—John Ruskin

INTRODUCTION

A rendering is considered by some to be a medium for transferring ideas from designer to client, a way to communicate what you have designed. However, many designers set their sights a little higher than that, because a presentation rendering is first and foremost a sales tool. Its job is to excite, stimulate, and maybe even inspire a client. Good presentation should be more than factual. It must have impact, and make a client want the proposed design.

Renderings are also one of the few tangible ways to keep the client entertained—and comforted by the wisdom of his choices—until the actual work is completed.

A quality, professional rendering is always built on the foundation of a carefully constructed perspective; no amount of gimmicks or flashy finishing touches can make a poorly done basic perspective layout look good. However, a well-conceived perspective drawing often lacks the appealing entourage elements that help to catch and hold a viewer's interest.

This book was developed to solve that problem. The collection of drawings of human figures and interior foliage is designed to make it as easy as possible to add the entourage components that enliven a rendering. A chapter of concentric ellipses from 7½ to 62½ degrees of inclination is included for assistance in the sometimes difficult task of drawing circular shapes in perspective.

Both interior designers and architects will find these reference drawings helpful, along with design students and commercial artists. Since the primary focus of the book is entourage elements for interior rendering, most of the tracing material is fitted to the presentation needs of an interior designer. However, a number of exterior situations, such as bicycling and sports, are included in the "People" chapter; and many drawings are suitable for both architectural and interior rendering applications.

OVERLEAF

This sketch was one of a series of design studies for a chain of airport shops. Since it was developed only to present a retail concept—not a finished design—the drawing was done in a loose, freehand style with lots of activity. PROJECT: Proposed Shop for Greyhound Leisure Services, Inc., Miami, FL; DESIGNER: Terranova Design Associates Inc.

THE TRACING FILES

Most renderings are done under a deadline, often a very difficult one. This book was designed to make fast work of finding appropriate entourage elements to add to your interior and architectural illustrations. Each tracing page has a cluster of reproductions of a drawing at several architectural scales, enabling quite a few drawings also to be used in presentation elevations. Many of the drawings are carefully redrawn at each scale (rather than photographically sized), with more detail in the large drawings and extensive simplification in the smaller-scale material, to make the tracing process easier. Each page is also marked at the side with a descriptive title and cross-referenced to other pages of possibly useful related material.

The pages are designed to be easily removed from the binding if you would like to add this material to your existing picture file system or start a new one. After removing the pages, they can be punched for a three-ring binder or sorted into file folders. If you prefer to keep the book intact in the binding, individual pages can be photocopied as needed— for tracing or to be cut up for further reproduction.

Although it is possible to start using the tracing files immediately without further instruction, this chapter outlines a number of techniques for using the drawings more effectively. A checklist is also provided at the back of the book, to be used as a desk-side reference while developing a rendering and as a tool to critique a finished picture.

△

Activity is the highlight of this illustration, which was done as part of a design proposal for the renovation of an old City of Miami fire station.   PROJECT: Proposed renovation of Firehouse #4, Miami, FL; DESIGNER: John Pierce Fullerton, AIA, Fullerton & Associates, Architect, Planners, Inc.

◁

An illustration of a model home interior usually emphasizes spaciousness and lifestyle more than furniture details, as this picture demonstrates. The viewpoint, looking through the kitchen pass-through to the living room and out the sliding glass door to the patio, shows off the visual spaciousness of an otherwise smallish unit. PROJECT: Pierpointe, a Spear Associates community, Pembroke Pines, FL; DESIGNER: Cano, Sotolongo & Associates Inc., Architects.

PHOTOCOPIERS

Office copiers are a useful drawing tool. They can handle a number of jobs that would be time-consuming if done by hand, such as enlargement or reduction of images to suit sizing needs.

A copier also makes left-to-right image reversal easier. An image "flop" is sometimes needed to position a drawing of a person so that it is facing in the correct direction for picture composition purposes. For example, it usually enhances a picture to have the key human figures in the rendering looking or moving toward the focal point. This can be accomplished by photocopying an image that needs left-to-right reversal on translucent vellum, then tracing through the back of the vellum onto the rendering layout. An alternative method is to photocopy the image on self-adhesive plastic film, and affix the film to the back of the rendering layout.

A photocopier can also pull together a number of images from different sources, which have been pasted together on a rendering layout, into a clean, seamless finished piece. The only disadvantage to this rendering shortcut is that a compilation of images from several sources composed into a single picture often lacks the visual continuity of a picture that has been drawn or traced by a single person.

PEOPLE

One of the easiest ways to make an illustration "come alive" is to add people to the picture. The human figure increases the impact of a rendering tremendously for a number of reasons.

First of all, people tend to evaluate images in human-scale terms. A correctly sized figure is the clearest way to communicate to your viewer the scale of a design. This can be especially important if there are unusually scaled elements in the rendering—such as an oversize sofa or a lofty ceiling. Without a human figure to establish scale relationships among the pictured elements, the unusually sized items can look vaguely disturbing or poorly drawn.

A person—just like a strategically placed potted palm—can also be used to cover up an area of the picture where the design details have not been worked out yet, or one that you simply do not have time to draw.

People can be used to convey the particular "look" or style of the design. A sophisticated, well-dressed couple being seated by a handsome maitre d' can help a sleek restaurant concept gain client approval. The dress, age, and general appearance of the people can set the tone for your picture—along with the activities they are engaged in. For example, a

People are often used in a rendering to tell a story about the buildings. Here, the children serve two purposes. First, they indicate that the project is family-oriented; and, second, their positioning—standing casually with their bikes in the cul-de-sac street—emphasizes the lack of auto traffic. PROJECT: Quatraine at Jacaranda, a Spear Associates community, Plantation, FL; DESIGNER: Cano, Sotolongo & Associates Inc., Architects.

This interior rendering of a model home was originally done without the man standing by the sofa. However, the client felt that the picture didn't effectively show the drama of the 17-foot high ceilings—possibly because the oversize windows created some distortion of scale relationships. The addition of the single human figure significantly changed the illustration, making the room appear much larger. PROJECT: Quatraine at Jacaranda, a Spear Associates community, Plantation, FL; DESIGNER: Cano, Sotolongo & Associates., Architects.

couple in tennis attire in a hotel lobby immediately indicates that there are tennis courts in the resort complex. Likewise, a scene with children playing will indicate a family-oriented project.

However, just as the right people at the best positions in a composition can vastly improve the picture, the wrong type of people—or, even worse, poorly drawn people—can ruin the effect of an otherwise fine rendering. Nothing destroys a picture faster than people that look wrong: with shoulders slumped forward, leering at the viewer with a strange smile, or strangely proportioned.

This is why some designers avoid putting figures in their renderings. An illustration usually looks better with no people in it at all than with poorly drawn, deformed figures. However, taking the time to draw attractive human figures and placing them appropriately in the picture pays big dividends in the quality of your finished rendering. And it's not difficult if you approach the problem properly.

PLACING PEOPLE IN A RENDERING

The first step in locating figures in a rendering is to select people from your tracing reference files that are appropriately dressed and posed to complement the design concept that is being presented. It is also helpful if they are engaged in activities that explain the proposed uses of the design.

Try to use figures in several different scales, possibly running the gamut from ¼" to foreground size, to create a greater illusion of depth in the illustration. The illusion of depth can be enhanced further by placing the figures in front of, or partially behind, or layered between other picture elements. This overlapping effect is a powerful device for creating a more dramatic picture.

Next, the figures should be positioned correctly in relation to the eye level (horizon line). Drawings of people must obey the same laws of perspective as other objects in a rendering. They should be scaled in proportion to the architecture and viewed from about the same eye level. An easy way to achieve this is to use an eye level of 5'-0" above the floor or main level of the rendering to develop the perspective layout. A 5'-0" horizon line approximates the normal eye level of the average woman and falls at about the bottom of the chin of the average man.

If you consider the horizon line as a clothesline and the human figures as paper cutouts, then you simply "hang" the women by their eyes and the men by their chins on this line. According to their size, wherever their feet touch the floor is where they are standing in the picture.

Of course, this five-foot eye-level method applies only to normal-size adults. People that are noticeably taller or shorter

A number of different entourage elements are positioned in this composition to pull the viewer's attention to the entrance doors. The perspective of the brick pavers and foreground car point to the entrance. Most of the people are either walking toward the entrance or away from it. The strong verticals created by the palm foliage on either side of the driveway tend to slow eye movement to the sides of the picture. PROJECT: Frenchman's Reef Resort, St. Thomas, V.I.; DESIGNER: Lynn Wilson Associates.

5'-0"

than average will have to hang slightly higher or lower than usual—for example, in the rendering of a professional basketball court—and children must be positioned using regular methods of height measurement.

This approach is especially effective when adding people in the extreme foreground of a picture. Even though only the upper torso is within the picture (as in many of the drawings marked "foreground" in the tracing files), a human figure is properly positioned when the very close figures hang by the same point on their anatomy as figures in the middle ground and background of the picture.

This technique of hanging people on the horizon line by a particular reference point on their anatomy can also be used with eye levels other than 5'-0"

Simply calculate the point on the figure that aligns with the eye level, and use that as a basis for sizing and positioning people within the picture. For example, a 6'-0" eye level would mean that the top of a man's head would hang at eye level, while a woman would stand slightly below eye level. Similarly, a 2'-0" eye level places the knees of adult figures at eye level.

For high eye levels, think of the figures as a fraction of the height from ground to horizon line. A 12'-0" eye level would mean that the male figures would be placed so that their overall height would equal half the distance from the bottom of their feet to the horizon line. (A higher eye level also requires that drawings of the figure be revised to reflect a higher angle of view, otherwise the people will look like they are tilting back in space).

USING PEOPLE IN A PICTURE COMPOSITION

The correct placement of people in a rendering in relation to eye level and scale of the architecture is important to the success of a rendering. Equally important is the need to position them in an effective and pleasing composition.

People are a compositional tool. A standing person is a vertical shape that can be used to slow down horizontal eye movement across a picture. A person or group of people can be used to balance a rendering that is too detailed on one side or the other or to enliven a static or boring section of the picture. Because the positioning of the people is not strictly dictated by the design layout—unlike the location of furniture, columns, windows, and other structural features—they are an especially versatile compositional tool for the artist.

As you look at the illustrations on these pages, notice how large, foreground-scale people are often used to frame the sides of a rendering, and that they usually face towards the focal point of the composition. This tends to keep the viewer from scanning the picture and exiting at the side, and leads the eye back to the center of the composition instead. Note also how clusters of people are used to "punctuate" left-to-right eye movement, creating stopping points and small compositions between the points.

FOLIAGE

One of the dictionary definitions of entourage is "surroundings," and occasionally a rendering has to be done in which the surroundings are not typical at all. The solution to a rendering problem like this neo-natal nursery is to do visual research on the appropriate entourage—such as Polaroid photos at the site, equipment catalogs, and sketch notes—before tackling the final picture. PROJECT: Sylvia Schwartz Neo-Natal Nursery, Mt. Sinai Medical Center, Miami Beach, FL; DESIGNER: Jerome Goebel, AIA.

People provide scale, activity, and interest to a rendering—but sometimes they are not appropriate to create the desired ambience. A human figure would only disrupt the calm elegance of this picture. PROJECT: Jonathan's Landing Condominium, Jupiter, FL; DESIGNER: Robert J. Shaw, ASID.

Interior foliage is another design element that can be useful in composing a rendering. Foliage softens the hard edges of architecture and adds color to the interior environment. Larger specimens can be used as a vertical accent for a room or to frame a picture composition at the side.

The pages of interior foliage in this book contain a collection of commonly used interior plants, sized at several scales, for use in both renderings and elevations. The drawings were created as entourage for interior rendering, not botanical reference material; the structure and stylization of leaf detail is simplified in many plants. Since foliage is often used in interior rendering only as a background or accessory item, extensive plant detail would only detract from the main design elements in a picture.

CIRCLES IN PERSPECTIVE

Circular shapes occur often in both interior and exterior renderings. The drawing of domes, arches, columns, and other curvilinear architectural shapes requires a clear understanding of how to use ellipses to represent circles in perspective. Smaller design details, such as lampshades, ashtrays, and circular tabletops, present a similar drawing problem.

The first step in drawing any of these circular forms is based on the concept in plane geometry that a circle can be fitted into any given square, with points of tangency at the midpoint of the sides of the square. The same principle is simply applied in perspective, creating an ellipse within a foreshortened square in perspective. As the square is tilted further away from the viewer in perspective, the ellipses that are formed become progressively narrower *(see Figure 1)*.

An ellipse is analyzed in geometry by two lines through its center, which are always perpendicular to each other. They are called the major and minor axes, and are an ellipse's longest and shortest dimensions *(see Figure 2)*.

It is important to understand these terms because the minor axis plays an important role in the process of positioning an ellipse. After a perspective square has been drawn and an

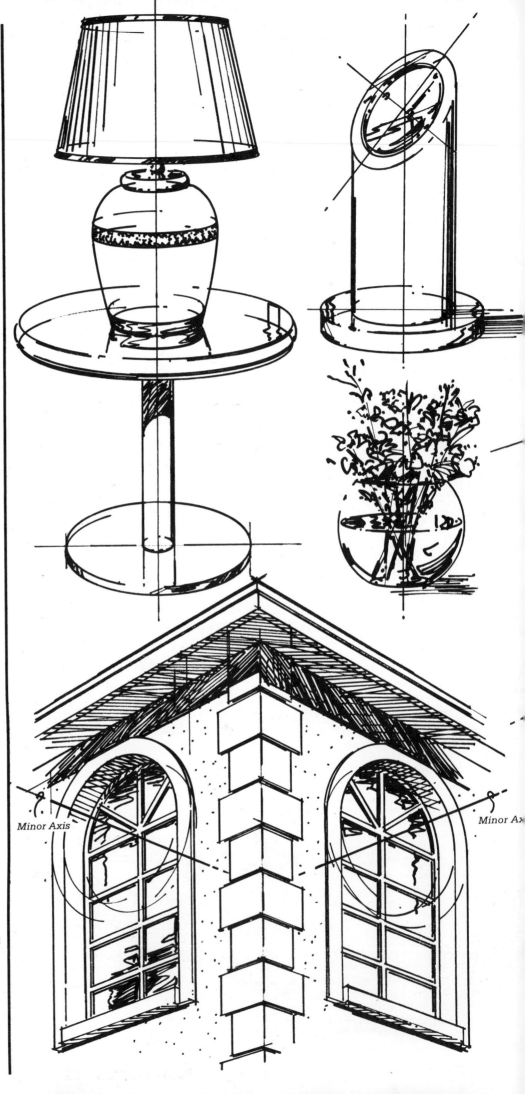

Minor Axis

Minor Ax

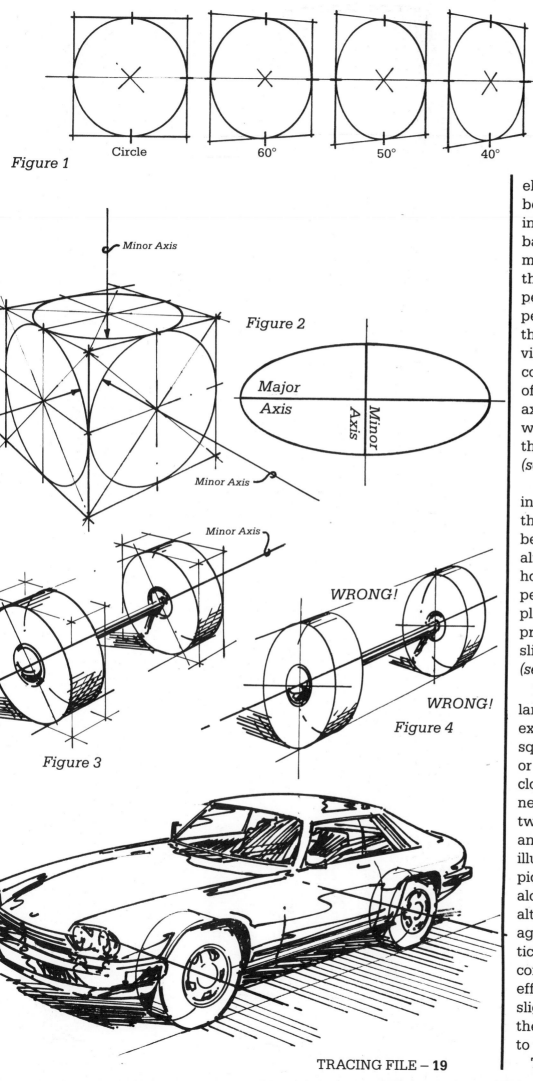

Figure 1

Circle   60°   50°   40°   30°   20°   10°

Minor Axis

Figure 2

Major Axis

Minor Axis

Minor Axis

Minor Axis

WRONG!

WRONG!

Figure 4

Figure 3

ellipse that fits within it has been selected from the "Circles in Perspective" section at the back of this book, the minor axis must be aligned with a line through the center of the perspective square that is perpendicular to the plane of the square. A simple way to visualize and remember this concept is to think of it in terms of a wheel and axle: the minor axis of an ellipse used to draw a wheel must align with the axle through the center of the wheel *(see Figure 3)*.

This principle may seem incorrect at first reading, and there is a tendency among beginning students to simply align the minor axis with a horizontal line when the perspective circle is in a vertical plane. However, this often produces ellipses that look slightly askew and "wrong" *(see Figure 4)*.

If an illustration requires a large circular shape within an extremely foreshortened square, such as a theater dome or round swimming pool from a close viewpoint, it may be necessary to splice together two ellipses of slightly different angles to create the proper illusion of depth within the picture. The ellipses are joined along their major axis and—although this method may not agree with the pure mathematical theories of ellipse construction—the desired effect of depth is created by slightly flattening the far side of the perspective circle in relation to the near side.

The tracing file of ellipses in

An accurately drawn prestige car enhances the perceived status of a home design rendering—if the car is affordable to the prospective home buyers and fits into their lifestyle. Although cars are not part of the focus of this book, they are an effective entourage item in many exterior renderings. PROJECT: Quatraine at Jacaranda, a Spear Associates community; DESIGNER: Cano, Sotolongo & Associates Inc., Architects.

this book was generated photographically and is easier to work with in drawings that require large circles in perspective than ellipses constructed by geometric methods—such as the ones used in many templates. Because their axes intersect at a foreshortened perspective center of the ellipse (rather than the geometric center), they are less complicated to position within the perspective squares used here as a construction device.

One final note about using ellipses in rendering: although the theory of drawing circles in perspective is mathematical and exact, in actual practice a certain amount of trial-and-error is involved. An ellipse that doesn't quite fit properly can often be turned slightly, or enlarged or reduced a fraction to align with its points of tangency on the perspective square that encloses it. These small adjustments may make an ellipse theoretically incorrect. Yet as long as it is fundamentally sized and positioned as outlined here, the drawing will be fine. There is an overriding principle in all drawing that if the image looks correct it is correct, and if it looks wrong it is wrong.

Hanging baskets and raised planters add foliage to this fast-food restaurant without wasting valuable floor area. PROJECT: Interior Concept for Burger King Restaurants; DESIGNER: Richard Cipolla, Bastian-Blessing Design.

People frame and control left-to-right eye movement in this sales rendering of the entry to an athletic club. Notice how the groupings of people lead the eye from reception desk to pro shop to racquetball court and seating grouping. Finally, a large foreground plant pulls the eye forward and stops the strong left-to-right perspective. PROJECT: Downtown Athletic Club, Miami, FL; DESIGNER: Gensler and Associates / Architects / Houston.

It was necessary to establish a viewpoint far enough away from the entrance of this airport lounge to encompass the entire area of the project. However, that left only a large, bland area of concourse carpet for the foreground. People were used to create interest and movement along the concourse. They also frame the composition on the left and right. PROJECT: Proposed Dobb's Airport Lounge, Miami International Airport; DESIGNER: Barry K. Slack, Robison & Associates, Inc., Interior Architecture.

Few things make a business owner happier than to see people buying his merchandise and cheerfully carrying it out of the store. This simple insight can be easily incorporated into a retail design presentation. PROJECT: Ship's Store at Pier 66 Resort, Ft. Lauderdale, FL; DESIGNER: Mary MacDonald, MacDonald Design Group.

½" = 1'

1" = 1'

⅜" = 1'

¾" = 1'

¼" = 1'

PREVIOUS PAGE

The tropical floral arrangement on the foreground table in this party room separates the rendering into two different vistas for the viewer's eye to follow. One side leads the eye back to the dancers and bartender, and the other leads out to the terrace and beyond. PROJECT: Portsview Condominium, Party Room, Miami, FL; DESIGNER: Robert M. Swedroe, AIA.

1½" = 1'

⅜" = 1'

¾" = 1'

½" = 1'

¼" = 1'

1" = 1'

$\frac{1}{4}'' = 1'$

$\frac{1}{2}'' = 1'$

$\frac{1}{2}'' = 1'$

$1'' = 1'$

$\frac{1}{4}'' = 1'$

$1'' = 1'$

$\frac{3}{4}'' = 1'$

$\frac{3}{4}'' = 1'$

$\frac{3}{8}'' = 1'$

$\frac{3}{8}'' = 1'$

1″ = 1′

½″ = 1′

⅜″ = 1′

¼″ = 1′

¾″ = 1′

BEDROOM - PEOPLE

also see pages 42 and 43

NOT TO SCALE

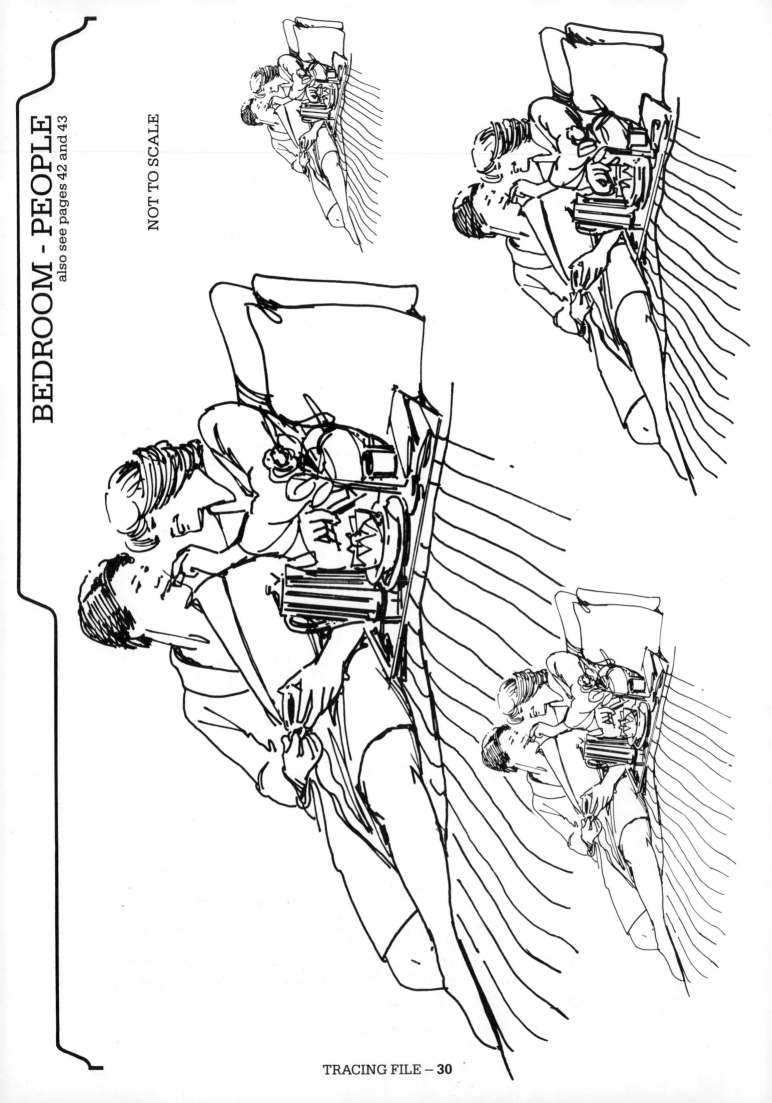

These breakfast trays are interchangeable with the one on the opposite page. They can also be used alone to add interest to a bedroom scene.

¾″ = 1′

¾″ = 1′

¼″ = 1′

1″ = 1′

½″ = 1′

1½″ = 1′

½″ = 1'

¼″ = 1'

1″ = 1'

1½″ = 1'

⅜″ = 1'

¾″ = 1'

3/4″ = 1′

3/4″ = 1′

3/8″ = 1′

3/8″ = 1′

1/2″ = 1′

1/4″ = 1′

1″ = 1′

¼" = 1'

1" = 1'

½" = 1'

⅜" = 1'

¼" = 1'

¾" = 1'

½" = 1'

1" = 1'

TRACING FILE – 35

ART CENTER COLLEGE OF DESIGN LIBRARY
1700 LIDA STREET
PASADENA, CALIFORNIA 91103

3/8" = 1'

1/2" = 1'

1/4" = 1'

3/4" = 1'

1" = 1'

3/4" = 1'

1/2" = 1'

1/4" = 1'

3/8" = 1'

1" = 1'

1½" = 1'

3/4" = 1'

1/2" = 1'

3/8" = 1'

1/4" = 1'

1" = 1'

½″ = 1′

¼″ = 1′

¼″ = 1′

1″ = 1′

1″ = 1′

3/8" = 1'

1/2" = 1'

3/4" = 1'

3/8" = 1'

3/4" = 1'

½″ = 1′

¾″ = 1′

⅜″ = 1′

1″ = 1′

¼″ = 1′

1½″ = 1′

¼″ = 1′

⅜″ = 1′

½″ = 1′

¾″ = 1′

1″ = 1′

1″ = 1′

¾″ = 1′

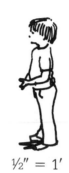

½″ = 1′

⅜″ = 1′

¼″ = 1′

¼″ = 1′

⅜″ = 1′

½″ = 1′

¾″ = 1′

1″ = 1′

1″ = 1′

¾″ = 1′

½″ = 1′

⅜″ = 1′

¼″ = 1′

NOT TO SCALE

NOT TO SCALE

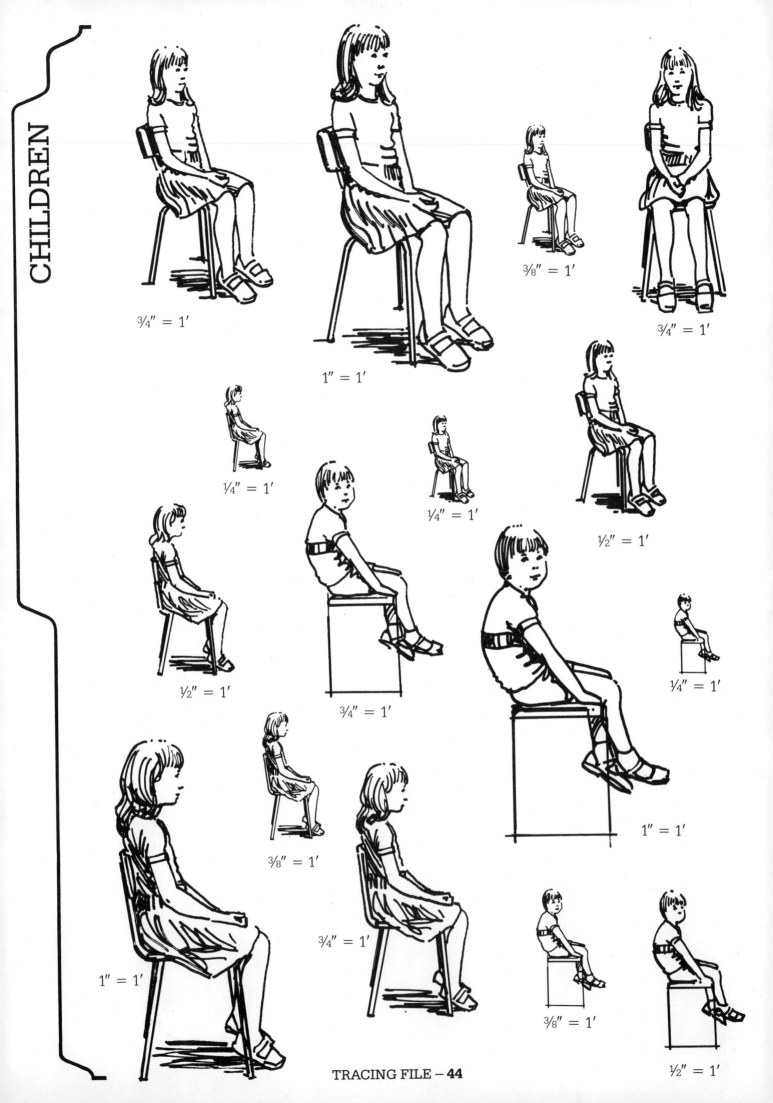

CHILDREN

¾″ = 1′

1″ = 1′

⅜″ = 1′

¾″ = 1′

¼″ = 1′

¼″ = 1′

½″ = 1′

½″ = 1′

¾″ = 1′

1″ = 1′

¼″ = 1′

1″ = 1′

⅜″ = 1′

¾″ = 1′

⅜″ = 1′

½″ = 1′

3/8″ = 1′

1/2″ = 1′

1/4″ = 1′

1/2″ = 1′

3/4″ = 1′

3/8″ = 1′

1/4″ = 1′

1″ = 1′

1″ = 1′

3/8″ = 1′

1/4″ = 1′

1/2″ = 1′

3/4″ = 1′

3/4″ = 1′

1/2″ = 1′

3/4″ = 1′

1/4″ = 1′

1″ = 1′

1″ = 1′

1/2″ = 1′

1″ = 1′

1/2″ = 1′

1/2″ = 1′

1″ = 1′

3/4″ = 1′

3/4″ = 1′

¼″ = 1′

⅜″ = 1′

½″ = 1′

¾″ = 1′

1″ = 1′

1″ = 1′

¾″ = 1′

½″ = 1′

⅜″ = 1′

¼″ = 1′

¼″ = 1′

⅜″ = 1′

½″ = 1′

¾″ = 1′

1″ = 1′

1″ = 1′

¾″ = 1′

½″ = 1′

⅜″ = 1′

¼″ = 1′

1″ = 1′

½″ = 1′

¼″ = 1′

¾″ = 1′

3/8″ = 1′

1½″ = 1′

1″ = 1′

½″ = 1′

1½″ = 1′

3/8″ = 1′

¼″ = 1′

¾″ = 1′

¼″ = 1′

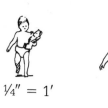

⅜″ = 1′

½″ = 1′

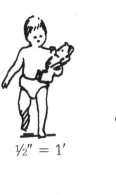

¾″ = 1′

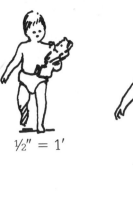

1″ = 1′

1″ = 1′

¾″ = 1′

½″ = 1′

⅜″ = 1′

¼″ = 1′

¼″ = 1′

⅜″ = 1′

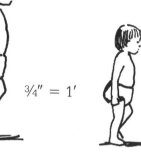

½″ = 1′

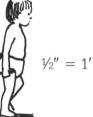

¾″ = 1′

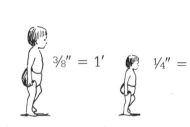

1″ = 1′

1″ = 1′

¾″ = 1′

½″ = 1′

⅜″ = 1′

¼″ = 1′

¾″ = 1′

⅜″ = 1′

½″ = 1′

⅜″ = 1′

¼″ = 1′

1½″ = 1′

½″ = 1′

1″ = 1′

¼″ = 1′

1½″ = 1′

¾″ = 1′

1″ = 1′

NOT TO SCALE

¾″ = 1′

¼″ = 1′

⅜″ = 1′

½″ = 1′

1″ = 1′

¼″ = 1′

⅜″ = 1′

1″ = 1′

¾″ = 1′

½″ = 1′

3/4″ = 1′

1/2″ = 1′

1/4″ = 1′

3/8″ = 1′

1″ = 1′

¼″ = 1′

¾″ = 1′

⅜″ = 1′

½″ = 1′

1″ = 1′

¼″ = 1′

⅜″ = 1′

¾″ = 1′

½″ = 1′

1″ = 1′

COUPLES – STANDING

¼″ = 1′

½″ = 1′

1″ = 1′

⅜″ = 1′

¾″ = 1′

1½″ = 1′

³⁄₄″ = 1′

³⁄₈″ = 1′

¼″ = 1′

½″ = 1′

¼″ = 1′

³⁄₄″ = 1′

1″ = 1′

³⁄₈″ = 1′

½″ = 1′

1″ = 1′

COUPLES — STANDING

3/8" = 1'

1/4" = 1'

1/2" = 1'

1" = 1'

3/4" = 1'

FOREGROUND

$\tfrac{3}{4}'' = 1'$

$\tfrac{1}{2}'' = 1'$

$\tfrac{3}{8}'' = 1'$

$1'' = 1'$

FOREGROUND

1″ = 1′

½″ = 1′

¼″ = 1′

¾″ = 1′

⅜″ = 1′

FOREGROUND

¼″ = 1′

1″ = 1′

½″ = 1′

¾″ = 1′

⅜″ = 1′

½″ = 1′

¾″ = 1′

¼″ = 1′

⅜″ = 1′

1″ = 1′

FOREGROUND

¼″ = 1′

¾″ = 1′

1″ = 1′

⅜″ = 1′

½″ = 1′

½″ = 1′

¼″ = 1′

¾″ = 1′

1″ = 1′

⅜″ = 1′

1" = 1'

½" = 1'

⅜" = 1'

¼" = 1'

¾" = 1'

3⁄8″ = 1′

1⁄4″ = 1′

1″ = 1′

3⁄4″ = 1′

1⁄2″ = 1′

DOGS

¼″ = 1′

⅜″ = 1′

½″ = 1′

¾″ = 1′

1″ = 1′

1″ = 1′

¾″ = 1′

½″ = 1′

⅜″ = 1′

¼″ = 1′

¼″ = 1′

⅜″ = 1′

½″ = 1′

¾″ = 1′

¼″ = 1′

⅜″ = 1′

½″ = 1′

¾″ = 1′

1″ = 1′

FOREGROUND

1″ = 1′

$1'' = 1'$

$3/8'' = 1'$

$3/4'' = 1'$

$1/4'' = 1'$

$1/2'' = 1'$

$1/4'' = 1'$

$3/4'' = 1'$

$3/8'' = 1'$

$1'' = 1'$

$1/2'' = 1'$

DOOR - PEOPLE

¾″ = 1′

½″ = 1′

1″ = 1′

1½″ = 1′

¼″ = 1′

⅜″ = 1′

½″ = 1′

¾″ = 1′

1″ = 1′

⅜″ = 1′

3/8" = 1'

1/2" = 1'

3/4" = 1'

1" = 1'

1/4" = 1'

¼″ = 1′

⅜″ = 1′

¾″ = 1′

1″ = 1′

½″ = 1′

¼″ = 1′

½″ = 1′

¾″ = 1′

⅜″ = 1′

1″ = 1′

HANDICAPPED – PEOPLE

¾″ = 1′

⅜″ = 1′

FOREGROUND

1″ = 1′

¼″ = 1′

½″ = 1′

½" = 1'

¾" = 1'

¼" = 1'

⅜" = 1'

1" = 1'

⅜" = 1'

¾" = 1'

¼" = 1'

½" = 1'

1" = 1'

¼" = 1'

½" = 1'

1" = 1'

⅜" = 1'

¾" = 1'

1½" = 1'

½″ = 1′

1″ = 1′

¾″ = 1′

⅜″ = 1′

¼″ = 1′

¼″ = 1′

½″ = 1′

1″ = 1′

⅜″ = 1′

¾″ = 1′

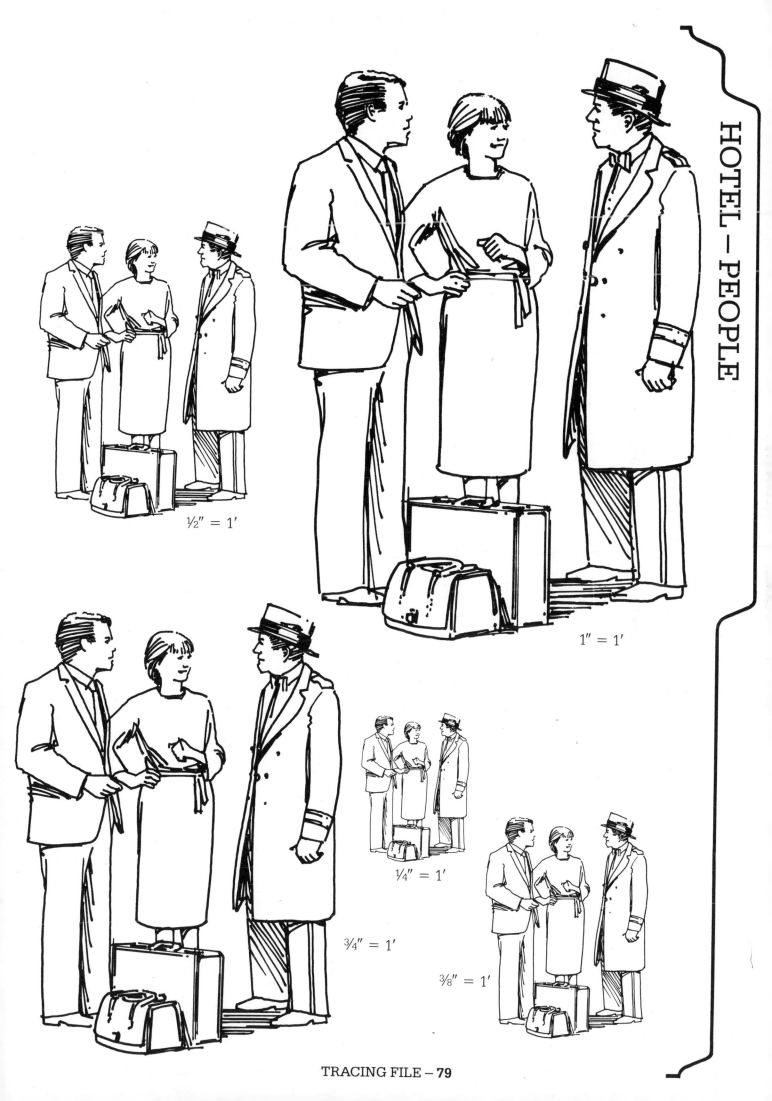

½″ = 1'

1″ = 1'

¾″ = 1'

¼″ = 1'

⅜″ = 1'

1″ = 1′

³⁄₈″ = 1′

³⁄₄″ = 1′

½″ = 1′

$\tfrac{3}{8}'' = 1'$

$1'' = 1'$

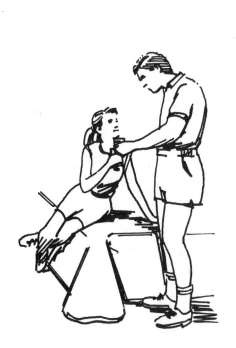

$\tfrac{1}{2}'' = 1'$

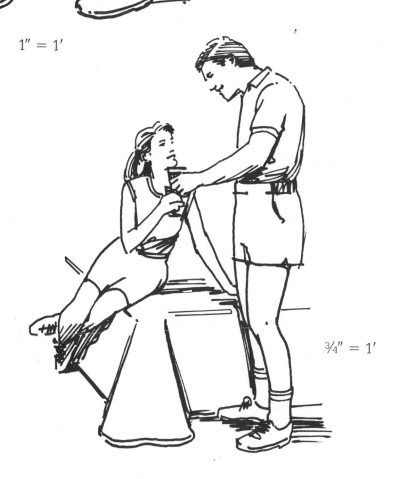

$\tfrac{3}{4}'' = 1'$

½″ = 1′

1″ = 1′

⅜″ = 1′

¼″ = 1′

¾″ = 1′

FOREGROUND

1″ = 1′

3⁄8″ = 1′

1⁄4″ = 1′

3⁄4″ = 1′

1⁄2″ = 1′

LIVING ROOM – PEOPLE

also see pages 42, 43, 102, 103, 194, and 195

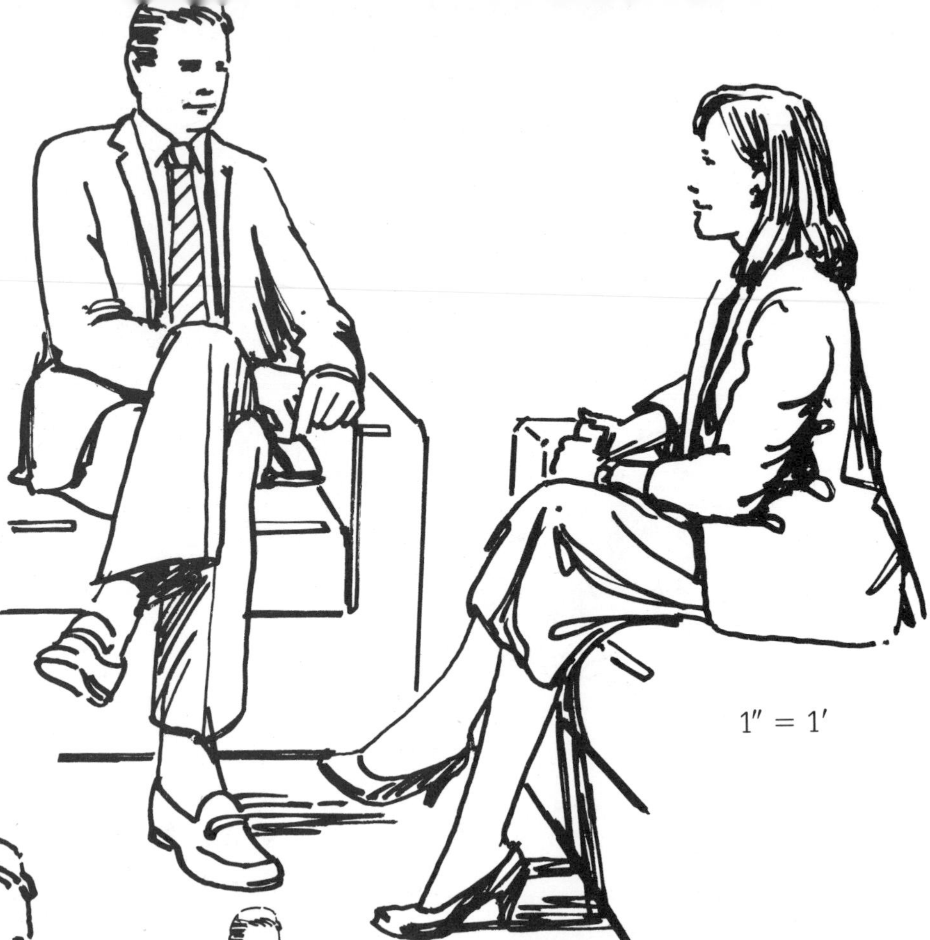

1″ = 1′

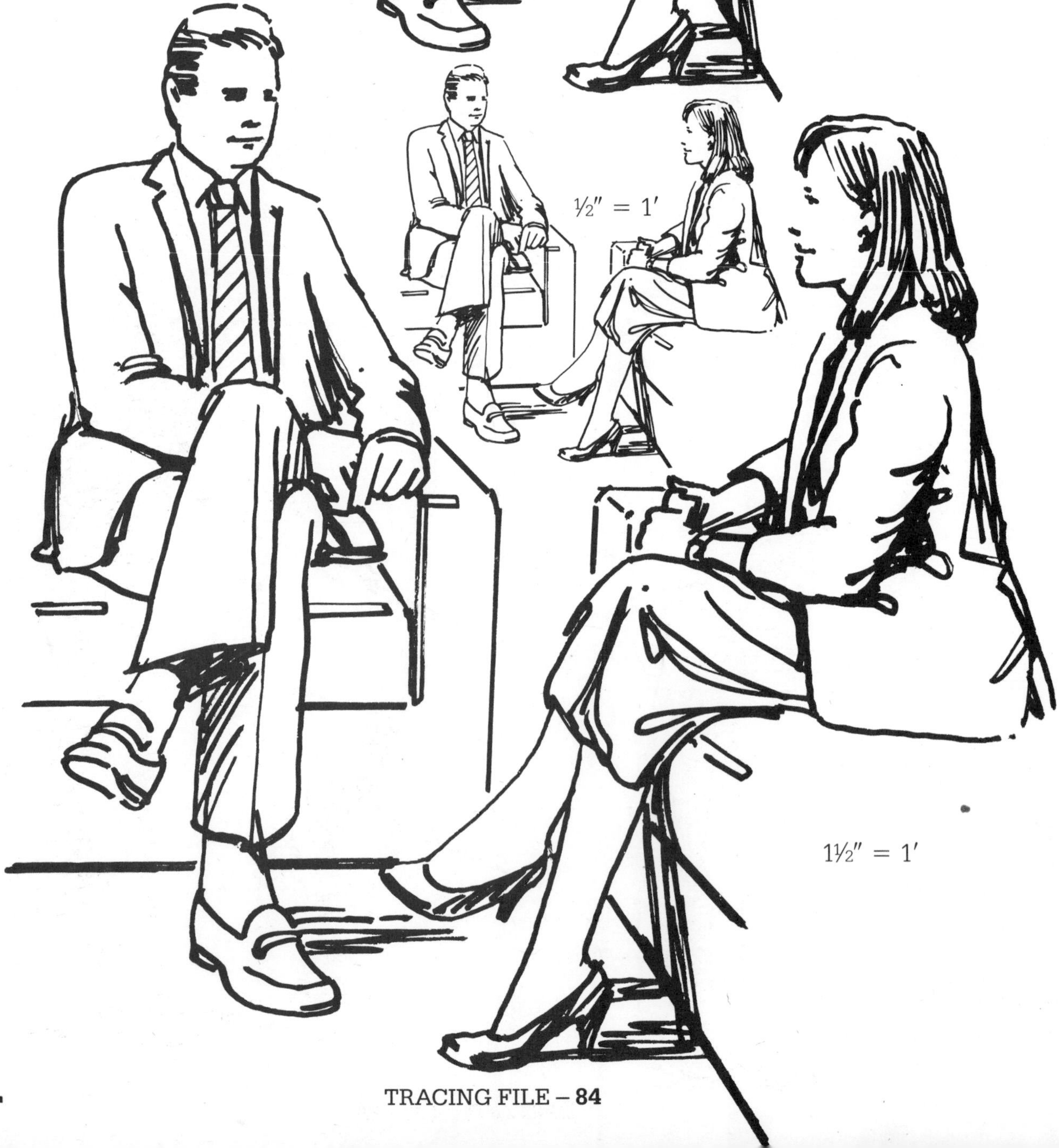

½″ = 1′

1½″ = 1′

3/8″ = 1′

1″ = 1′

3/4″ = 1′

1/4″ = 1′

1/2″ = 1′

3/4″ = 1′

3/8″ = 1′

1″ = 1′

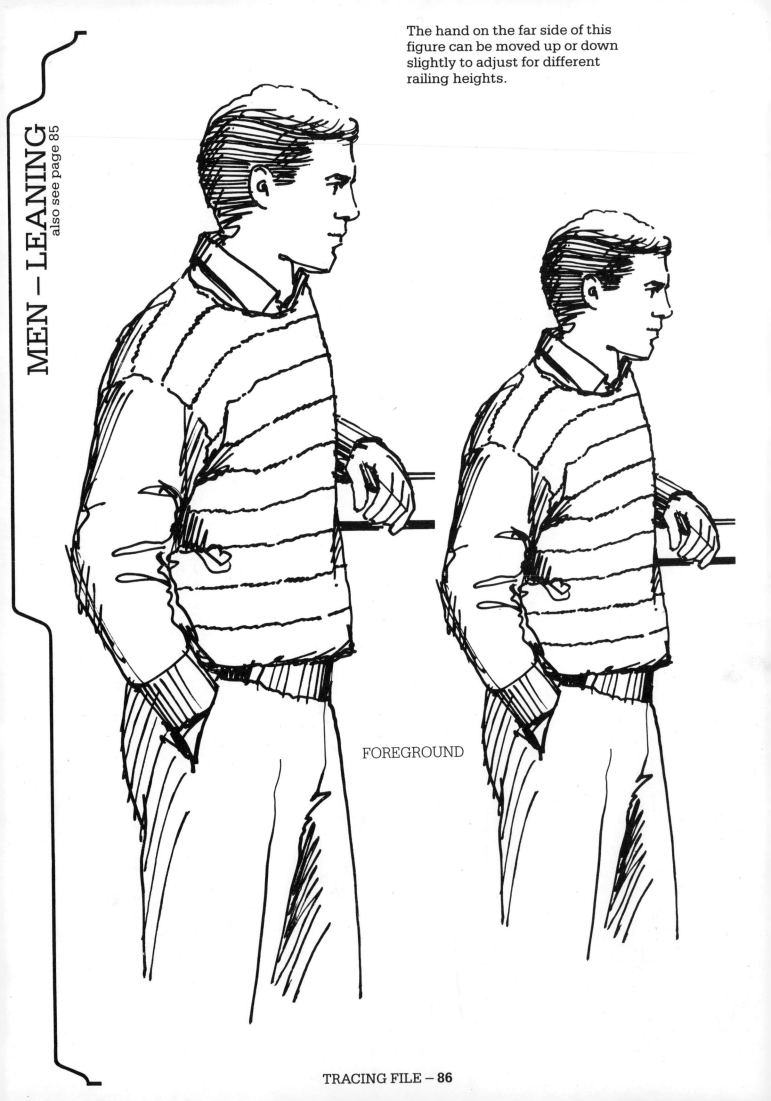

The hand on the far side of this figure can be moved up or down slightly to adjust for different railing heights.

FOREGROUND

¾″ = 1′

⅜″ = 1′

½″ = 1′

¼″ = 1′

1″ = 1′

½″ = 1′

1″ = 1′

¾″ = 1′

⅜″ = 1′

¼″ = 1′

32″

32″

32″

32″

32″

32″

¾″ = 1′

⅜″ = 1′

¼″ = 1′

½″ = 1′

1″ = 1′

1½″ = 1′

FOREGROUND

½″ = 1′

¾″ = 1′

1″ = 1′

⅜″ = 1′

¾″ = 1′

¼″ = 1′

⅜″ = 1′

1″ = 1′

½″ = 1′

¼″ = 1′

½″ = 1′

1″ = 1′

¼″ = 1′

1½″ = 1′

¾″ = 1′

⅜″ = 1′

1/4″ = 1′

1″ = 1′

1/2″ = 1′

3/4″ = 1′

3/8″ = 1′

1/2″ = 1′

3/4″ = 1′

1″ = 1′

1/4″ = 1′

3/8″ = 1′

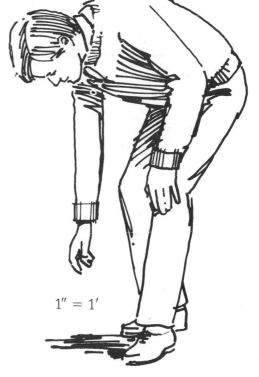

¼″ = 1′

¾″ = 1′

⅜″ = 1′

1″ = 1′

⅜″ = 1′

½″ = 1′

¾″ = 1′

¼″ = 1′

½″ = 1′

1″ = 1′

MEN - REACHING

¼″ = 1′

¾″ = 1′

½″ = 1′

⅜″ = 1′

1″ = 1′

1″ = 1′

½″ = 1′

¼″ = 1′

¾″ = 1′

⅜″ = 1′

MEN — SITTING

also see page 84

3/8″ = 1′

1″ = 1′

1/2″ = 1′

3/4″ = 1′

3/4″ = 1′

3/8″ = 1′

1/2″ = 1′

1/4″ = 1′

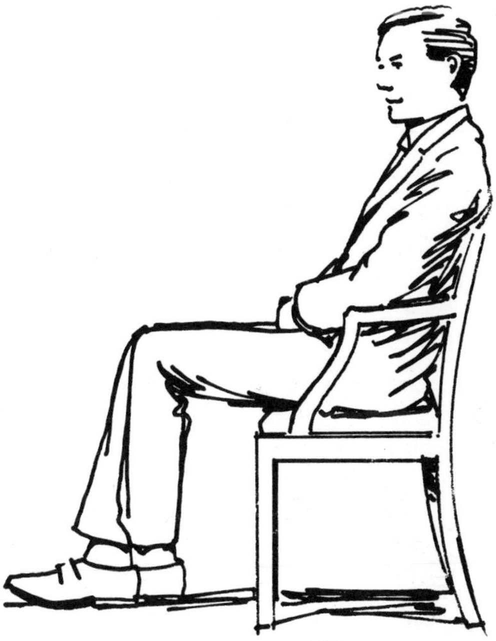

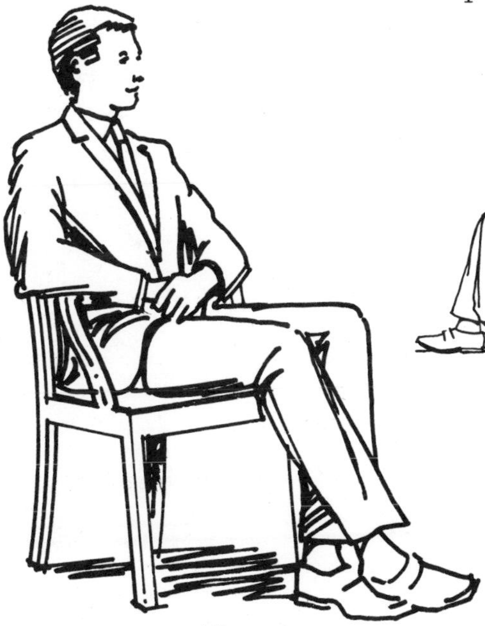

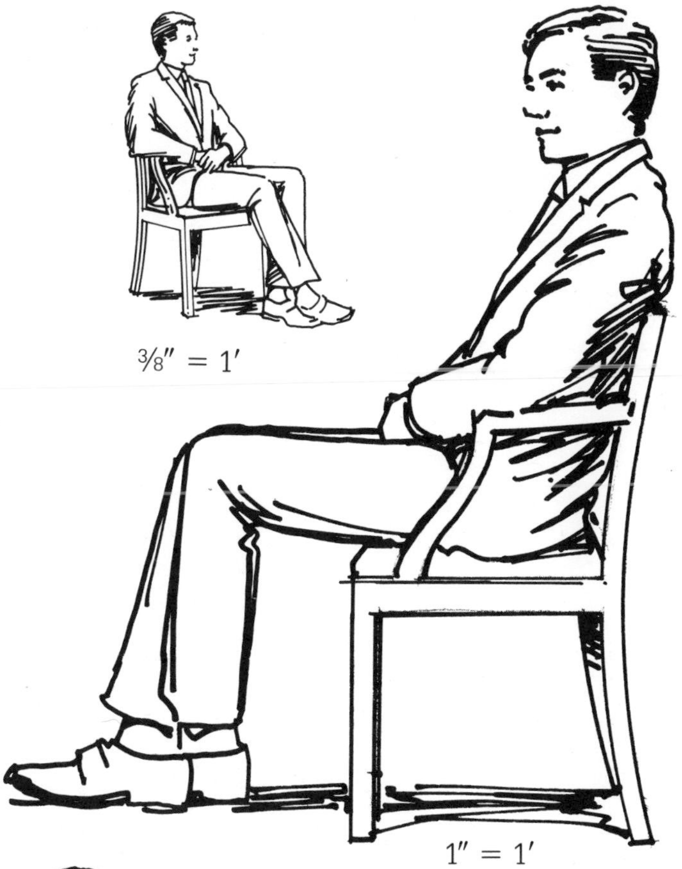

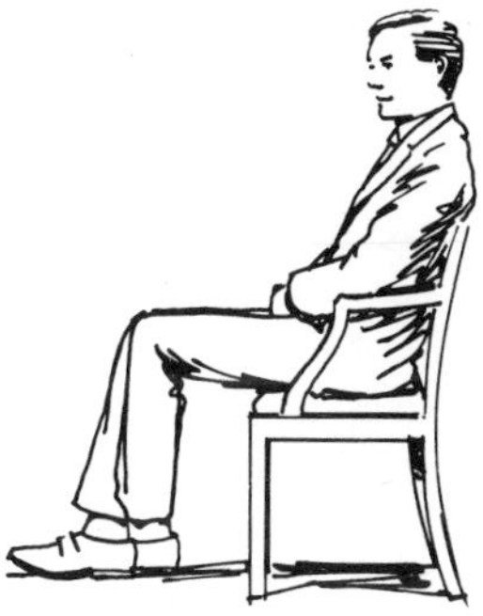

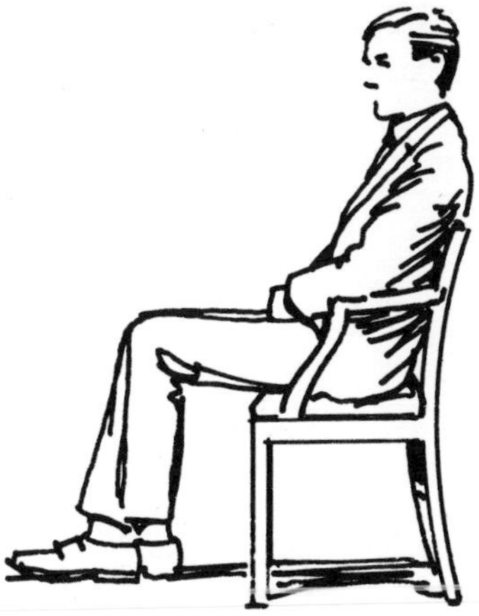

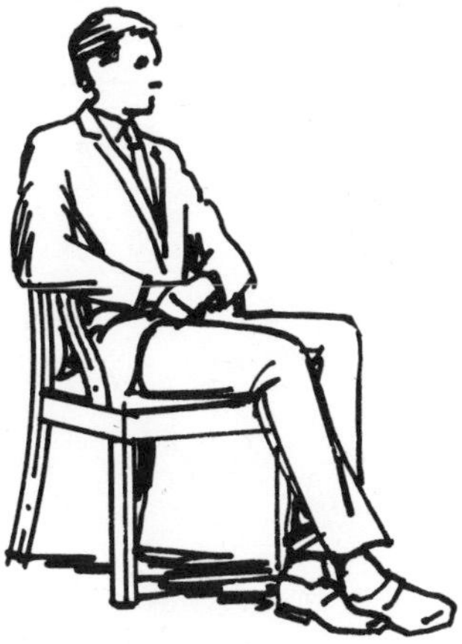

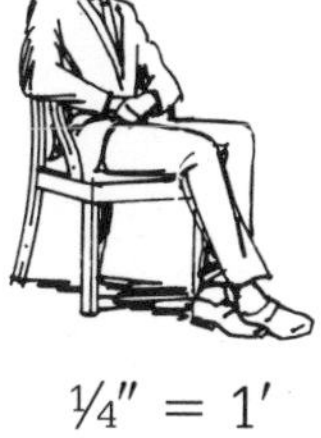

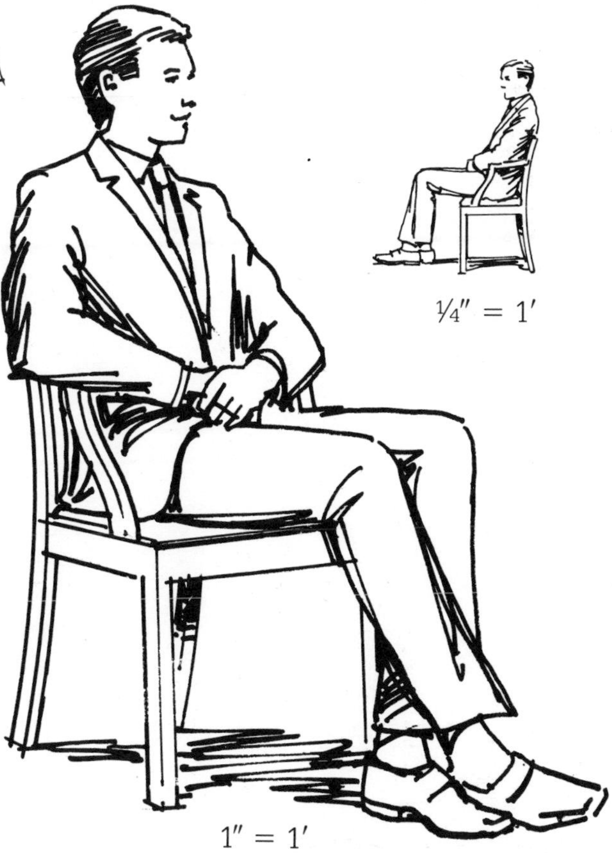

1/4″ = 1′

1″ = 1′

1″ = 1′

¼″ = 1′

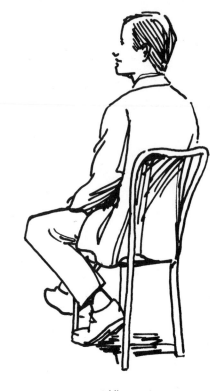

¾″ = 1′

½″ = 1′

⅜″ = 1′

½″ = 1′

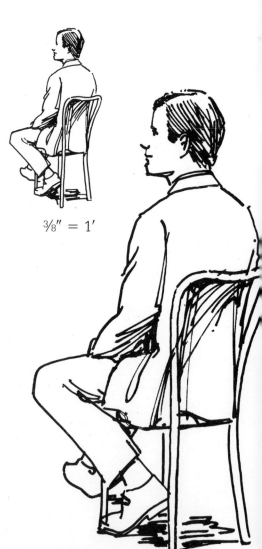

⅜″ = 1′

¾″ = 1′

¼″ = 1′

1″ = 1′

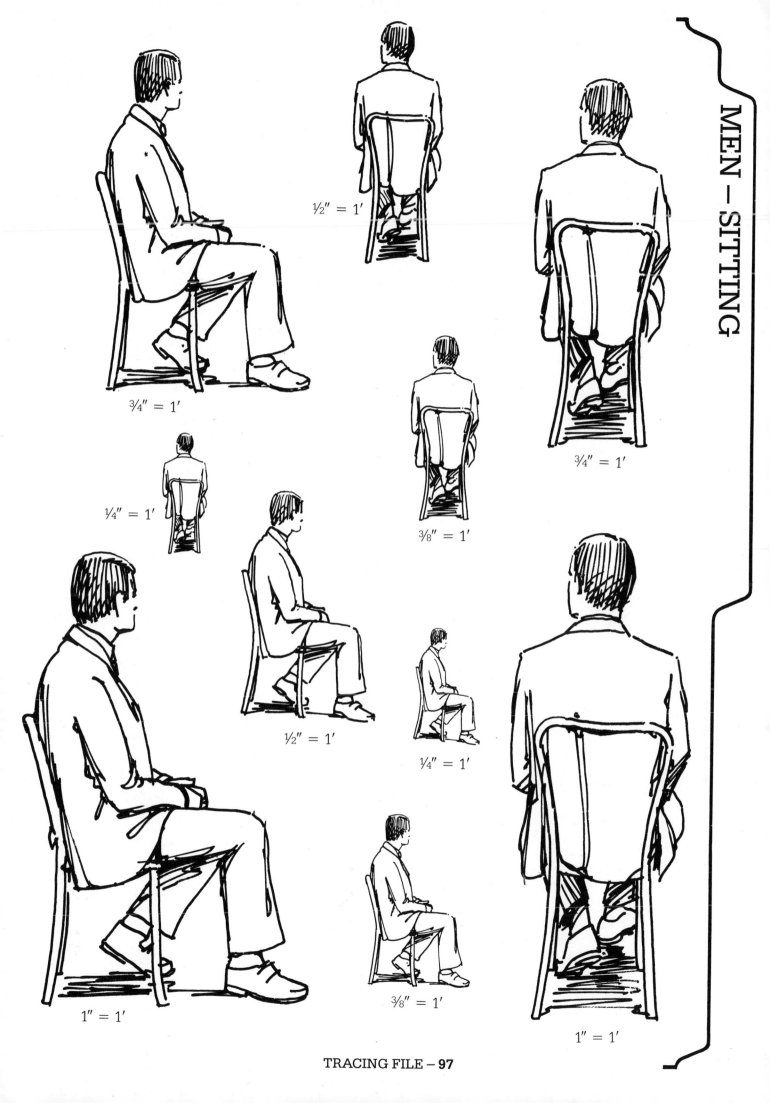

½″ = 1′

¾″ = 1′

¼″ = 1′

⅜″ = 1′

¾″ = 1′

½″ = 1′

¼″ = 1′

1″ = 1′

⅜″ = 1′

1″ = 1′

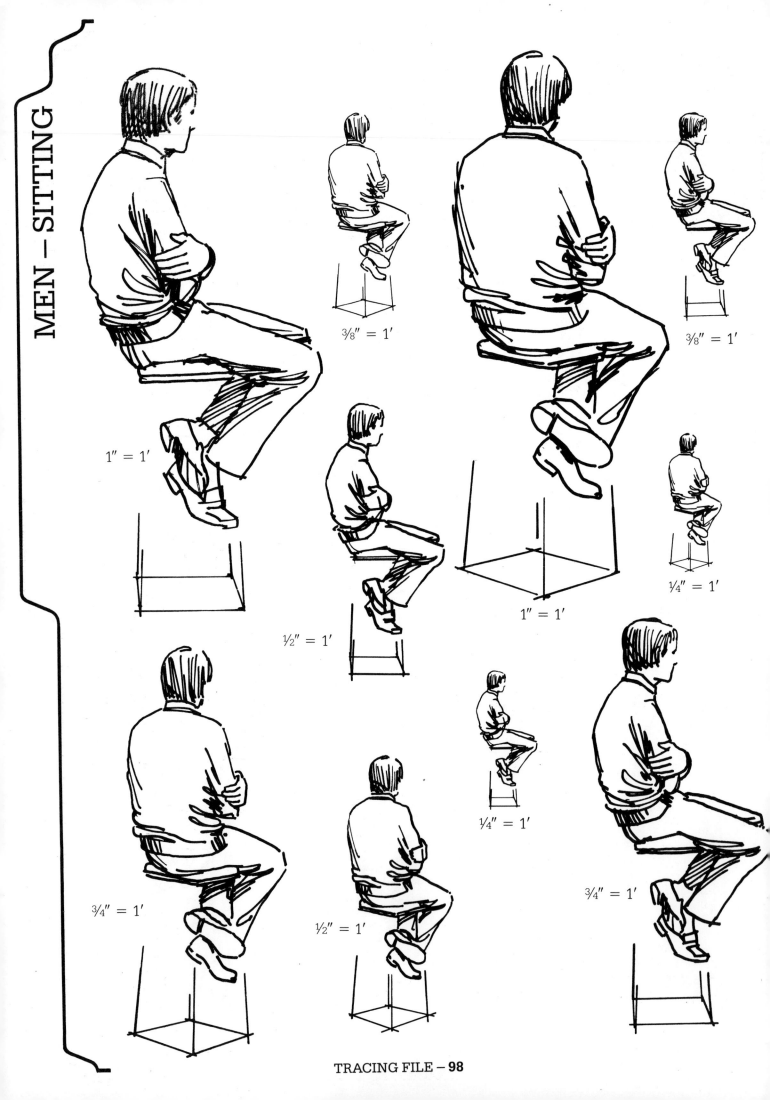

MEN – SITTING

1″ = 1′

3⁄8″ = 1′

3⁄8″ = 1′

1⁄2″ = 1′

1″ = 1′

1⁄4″ = 1′

3⁄4″ = 1′

1⁄2″ = 1′

1⁄4″ = 1′

3⁄4″ = 1′

TRACING FILE – 98

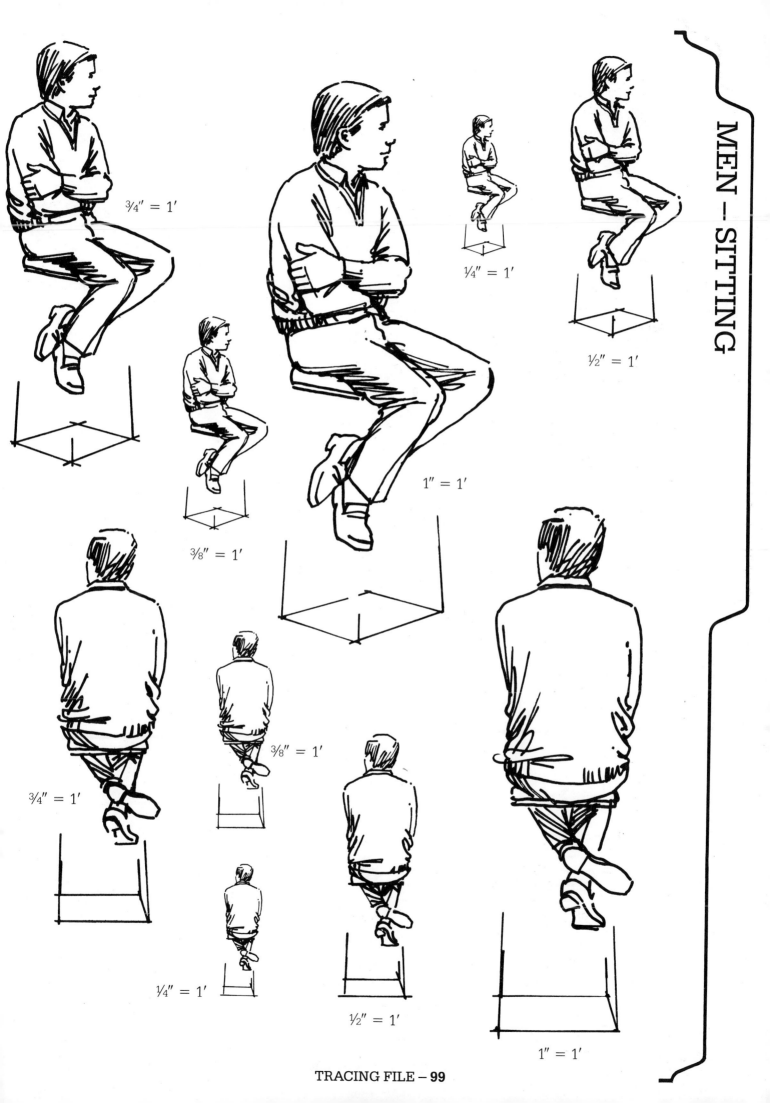

3/4″ = 1′

1/4″ = 1′

1/2″ = 1′

3/8″ = 1′

1″ = 1′

3/4″ = 1′

3/8″ = 1′

1/4″ = 1′

1/2″ = 1′

1″ = 1′

1″ = 1′

½″ = 1′

3⁄8″ = 1′

¼″ = 1′

¼″ = 1′

¾″ = 1′

1″ = 1′

¾″ = 1′

3⁄8″ = 1′

¾″ = 1′

½″ = 1′

¼″ = 1′

3⁄8″ = 1′

½″ = 1′

3⁄8″ = 1′

½″ = 1′

1″ = 1′

¾″ = 1′

1″ = 1′

3/8" = 1'

1/2" = 1'

1" = 1'

1/4" = 1'

3/4" = 1'

3/4" = 1'

3/8" = 1'

1" = 1'

1/4" = 1'

1/2" = 1'

¼" = 1'

³⁄₈" = 1'

½" = 1'

1" = 1'

¾" = 1'

1½" = 1'

½″ = 1′

1½″ = 1′

1″ = 1′

¾″ = 1′

⅜″ = 1′

¼″ = 1′

FOREGROUND

1″ = 1′

3/8″ = 1′

3/4″ = 1′

1/2″ = 1′

1/4″ = 1′

3/8" = 1'

1/2" = 1'

1/4" = 1'

1" = 1'

1" = 1'

1/4" = 1'

1/2" = 1'

3/8" = 1'

1 1/2" = 1'

3/4" = 1'

3/4" = 1'

$\frac{3}{8}'' = 1'$

$\frac{1}{2}'' = 1'$

$\frac{3}{4}'' = 1'$

$\frac{1}{4}'' = 1'$

$1'' = 1'$

$\frac{1}{4}'' = 1'$

$\frac{1}{2}'' = 1'$

$\frac{3}{8}'' = 1'$

$\frac{3}{4}'' = 1'$

$1'' = 1'$

¼″ = 1′

⅜″ = 1′

1″ = 1′

½″ = 1′

¾″ = 1′

1½″ = 1′

FOREGROUND

$\frac{3}{4}'' = 1'$

$\frac{1}{4}'' = 1'$

$\frac{3}{8}'' = 1'$

$1'' = 1'$

$1\frac{1}{2}'' = 1'$

$\frac{1}{2}'' = 1'$

1/4" = 1'

3/8" = 1'

3/4" = 1'

1/2" = 1'

1" = 1'

3/8" = 1'

1/4" = 1'

3/4" = 1'

1/2" = 1'

1" = 1'

1 1/2" = 1'

$3/8'' = 1'$

$1/4'' = 1'$

$3/4'' = 1'$

$1/4'' = 1'$

$1'' = 1'$

$1/2'' = 1'$

$1'' = 1'$

$3/4'' = 1'$

$3/8'' = 1'$

$1/2'' = 1'$

3⁄8″ = 1′

1″ = 1′

3⁄4″ = 1′

1⁄4″ = 1′

1⁄2″ = 1′

¾″ = 1′

⅜″ = 1′

¼″ = 1′

½″ = 1′

1½″ = 1′

1″ = 1′

$\frac{1}{2}'' = 1'$

$\frac{3}{4}'' = 1'$

$\frac{1}{4}'' = 1'$

$\frac{3}{8}'' = 1'$

$1'' = 1'$

$\frac{1}{4}'' = 1'$

$1'' = 1'$

$\frac{3}{8}'' = 1'$

$\frac{3}{4}'' = 1'$

$\frac{1}{2}'' = 1'$

$\frac{1}{2}'' = 1'$

$\frac{1}{4}'' = 1'$

$\frac{3}{8}'' = 1'$

$1'' = 1'$

$\frac{3}{4}'' = 1'$

$\frac{1}{2}'' = 1'$

$\frac{3}{4}'' = 1'$

$\frac{1}{4}'' = 1'$

½″ = 1′

¼″ = 1′

1″ = 1′

⅜″ = 1′

⅜″ = 1′

¾″ = 1′

1″ = 1′

3/8″ = 1′

3/4″ = 1′

1/4″ = 1′

1/2″ = 1′

1½″ = 1′

1″ = 1′

¼″ = 1′

½″ = 1′

¾″ = 1′

⅜″ = 1′

1″ = 1′

⅜″ = 1′

1″ = 1′

¼″ = 1′

¾″ = 1′

½″ = 1′

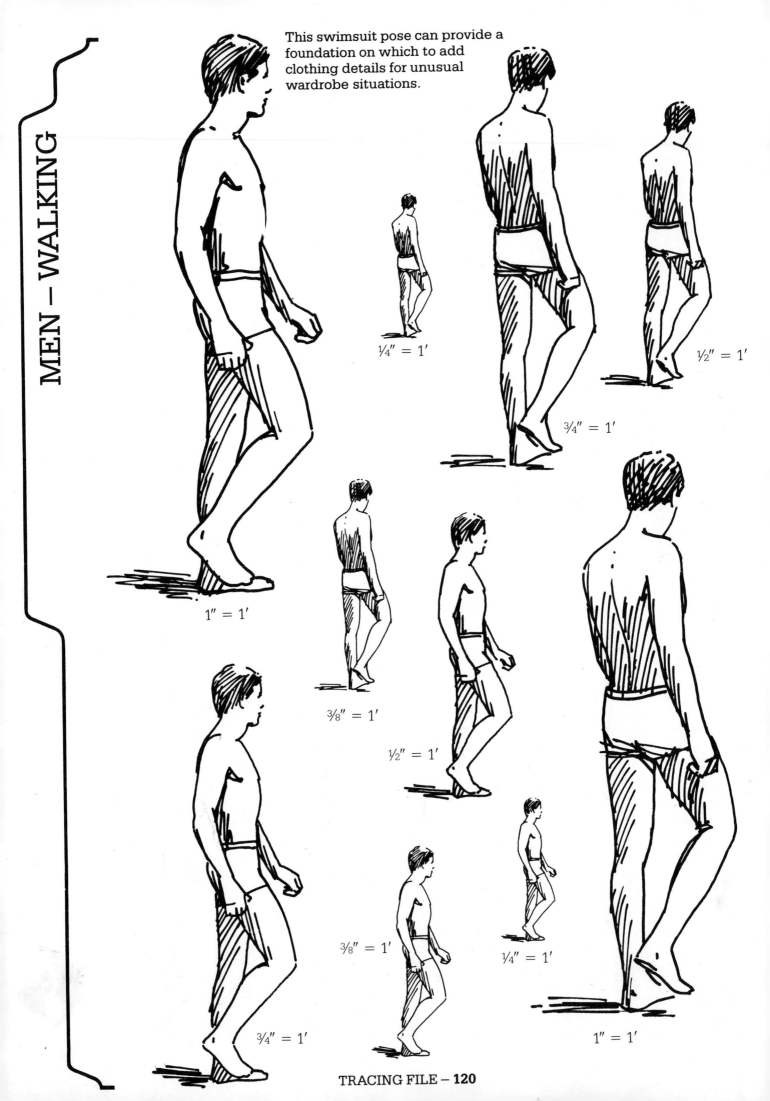

This swimsuit pose can provide a foundation on which to add clothing details for unusual wardrobe situations.

¼" = 1'

¾" = 1'

½" = 1'

1" = 1'

⅜" = 1'

½" = 1'

⅜" = 1'

¼" = 1'

¾" = 1'

1" = 1'

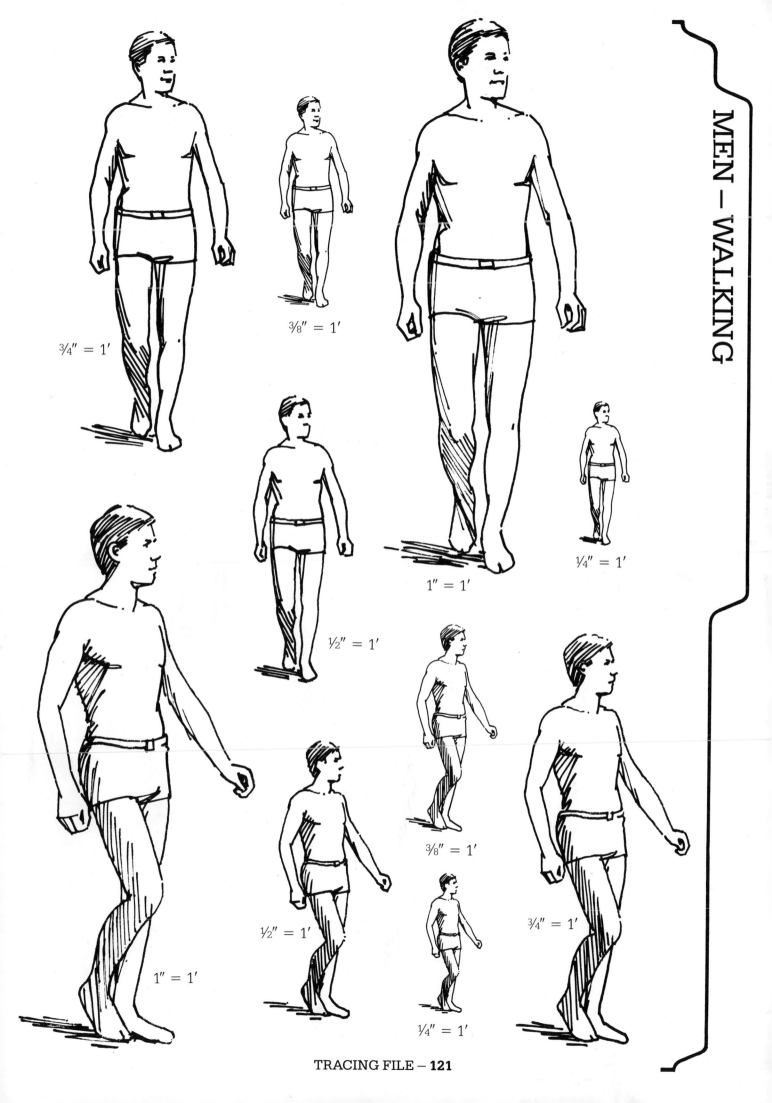

3/4″ = 1′

3/8″ = 1′

1/4″ = 1′

1″ = 1′

1/2″ = 1′

3/8″ = 1′

1/2″ = 1′

1″ = 1′

1/4″ = 1′

3/4″ = 1′

FOREGROUND

FOREGROUND

¾″ = 1′

1″ = 1′

¼″ = 1′

⅜″ = 1′

½″ = 1′

1½″ = 1′

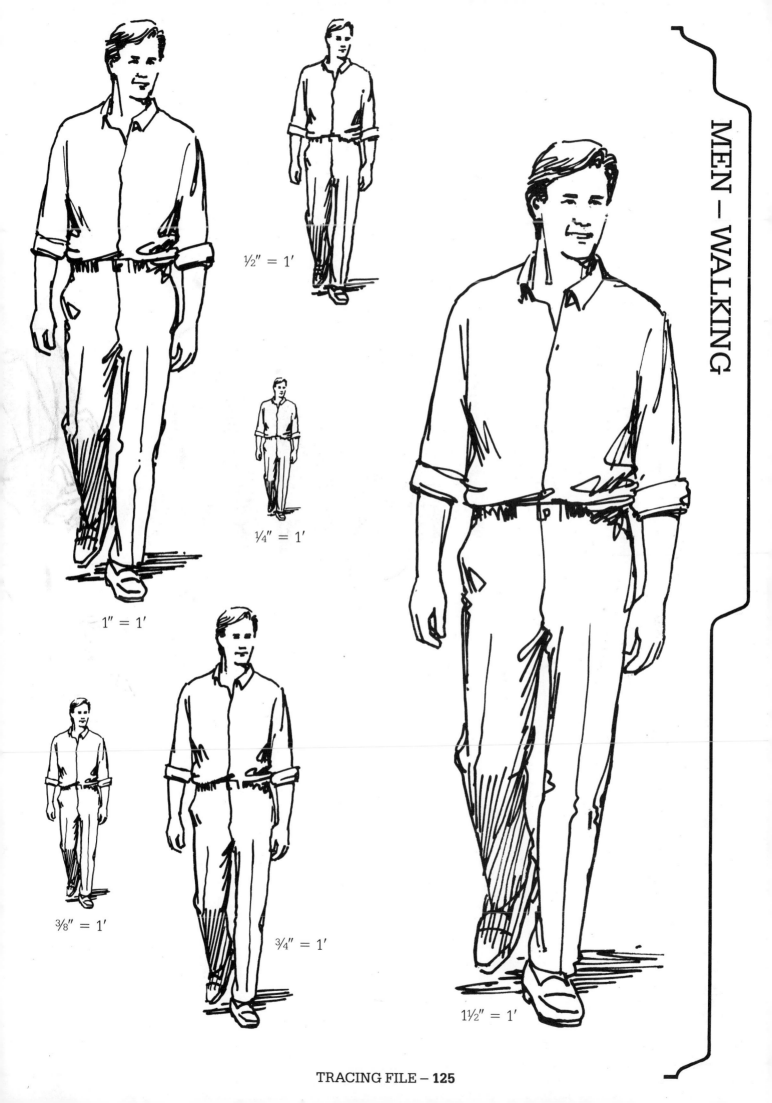

½″ = 1′

¼″ = 1′

1″ = 1′

⅜″ = 1′

¾″ = 1′

1½″ = 1′

$1\frac{1}{2}'' = 1'$

¾″ = 1′

¼″ = 1′

1″ = 1′

½″ = 1′

⅜″ = 1′

½″ = 1′

1″ = 1′

¾″ = 1′

¼″ = 1′

⅜″ = 1′

¼″ = 1′

¾″ = 1′

½″ = 1′

⅜″ = 1′

1″ = 1′

1″ = 1′

½″ = 1′

⅜″ = 1′

¾″ = 1′

¼″ = 1′

OFFICE — PEOPLE

also see pages 105, 112, 113, 116-19, 122-24, 126-29, 184-88, 199-203, 205-07, and 209

1½″ = 1′

¾″ = 1′

1″ = 1′

⅜″ = 1′

¼″ = 1′

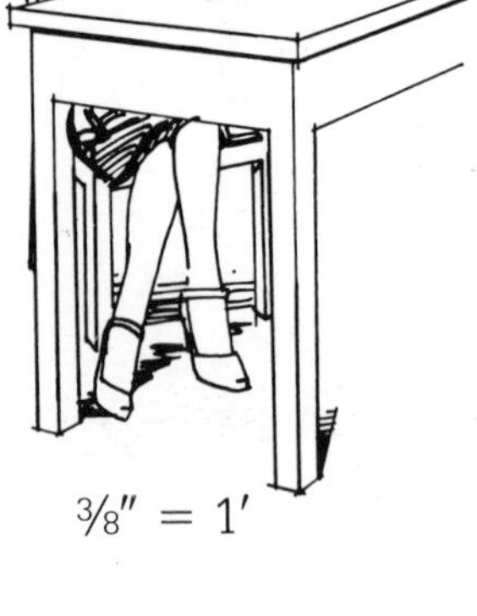

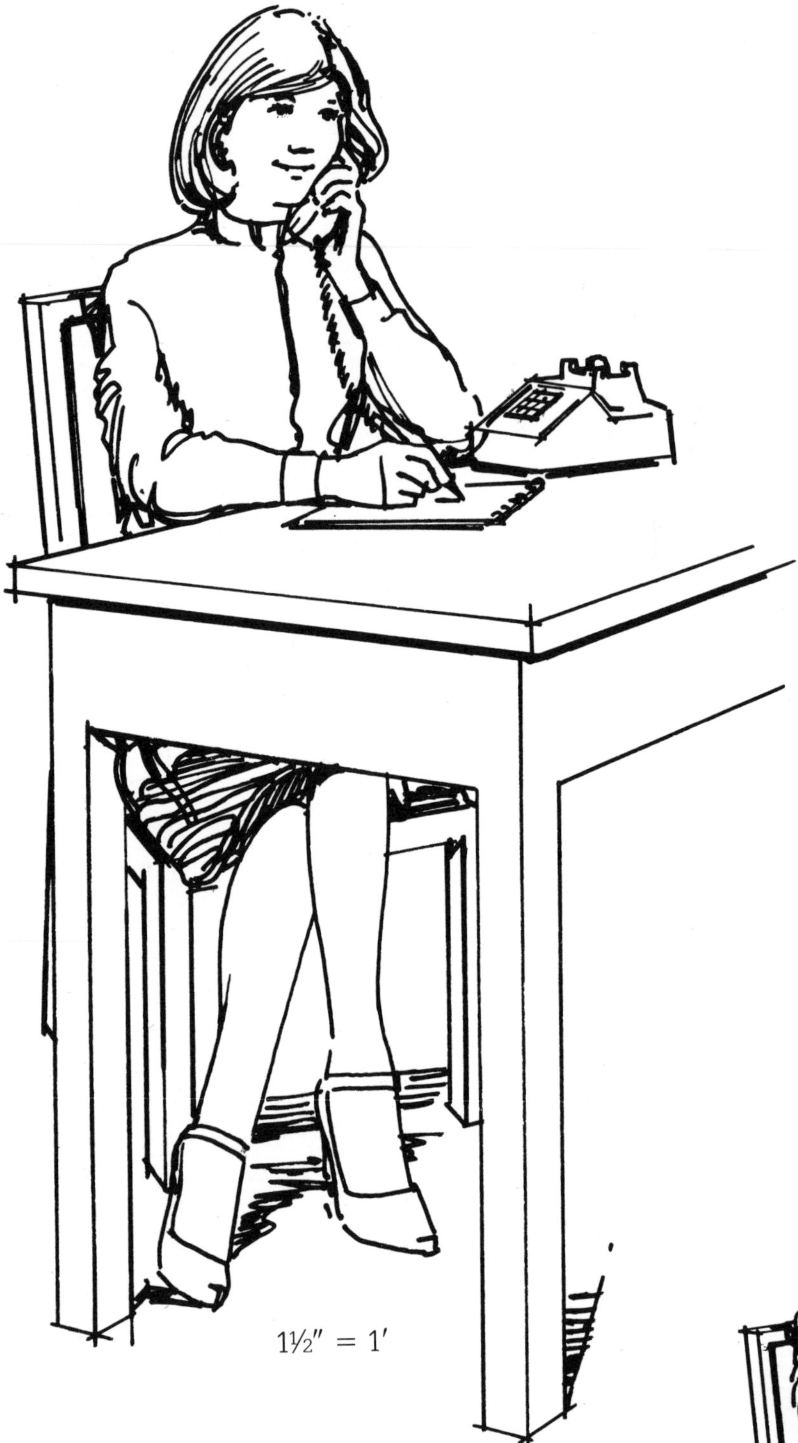

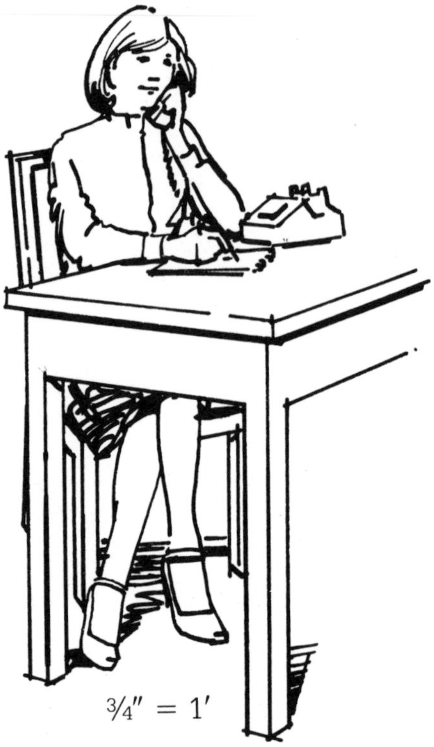

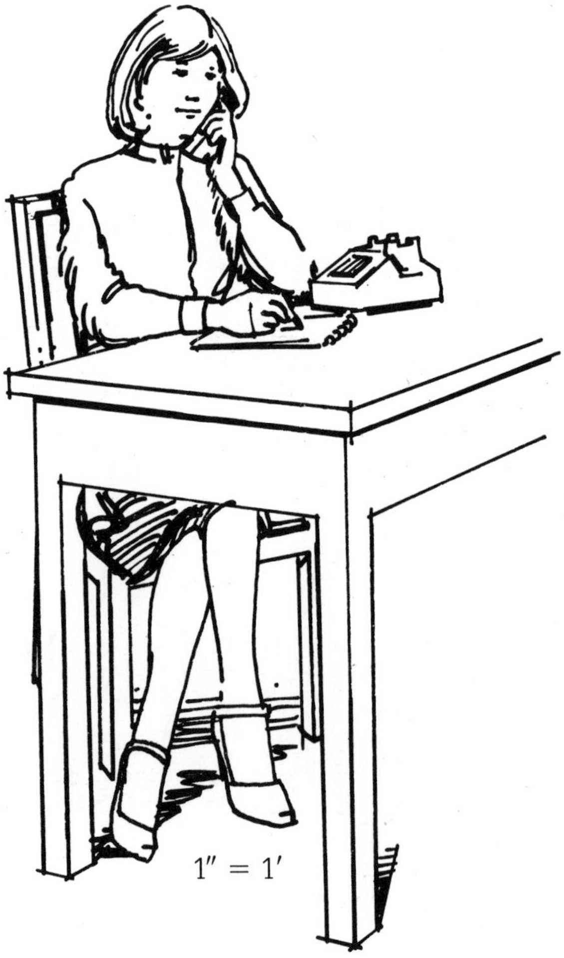

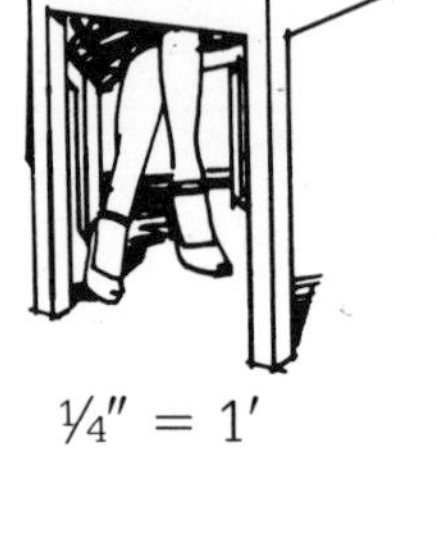

¼″ = 1′

⅜″ = 1′

½″ = 1′

¾″ = 1′

1″ = 1′

1½″ = 1′

1″ = 1′

½″ = 1′

⅜″ = 1′

¼″ = 1′

¾″ = 1′

FOREGROUND

$1'' = 1'$

$3/8'' = 1'$

$1/2'' = 1'$

$3/4'' = 1'$

$1/4'' = 1'$

$1/2'' = 1'$

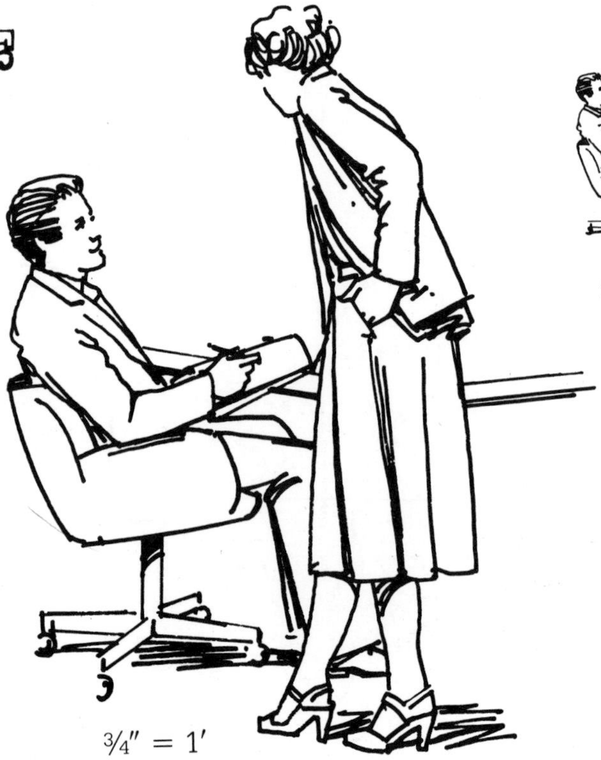

$3/4'' = 1'$

¼″ = 1′

¾″ = 1′

1″ = 1′

⅜″ = 1′

¼″ = 1′

½″ = 1′

1″ = 1′

⅜″ = 1′

3/8″ = 1′

1″ = 1′

3/4″ = 1′

1/4″ = 1′

1/2″ = 1′

FOREGROUND

3/8″ = 1′

1/4″ = 1′

3/4″ = 1′

1″ = 1′

FOREGROUND

1/2″ = 1′

¾″ = 1′

½″ = 1′

¼″ = 1′

FOREGROUND

1″ = 1′

⅜″ = 1′

½″ = 1′

¾″ = 1′

1″ = 1′

⅜″ = 1′

¼″ = 1′

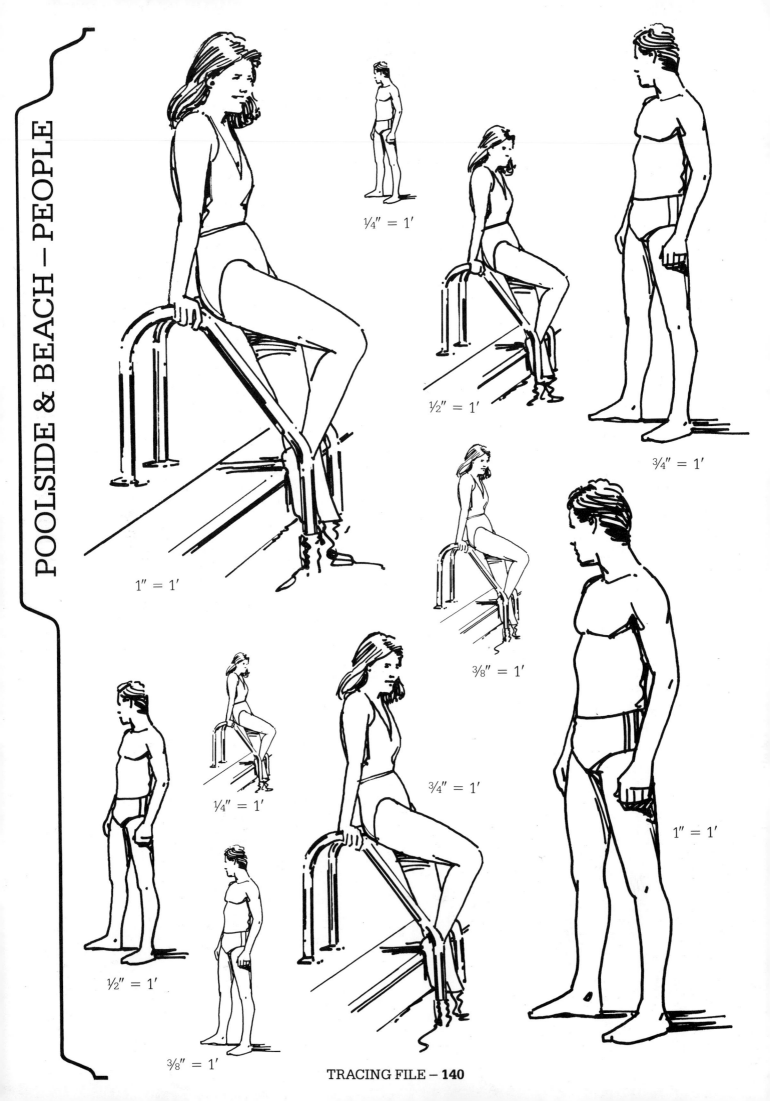

POOLSIDE & BEACH – PEOPLE

¼″ = 1′

½″ = 1′

¾″ = 1′

1″ = 1′

⅜″ = 1′

¼″ = 1′

¾″ = 1′

1″ = 1′

½″ = 1′

⅜″ = 1′

TRACING FILE – 140

NOT TO SCALE

POOLSIDE & BEACH – PEOPLE

½" = 1'

¾" = 1'

⅜" = 1'

¼" = 1'

1" = 1'

¾" = 1'

1½" = 1'

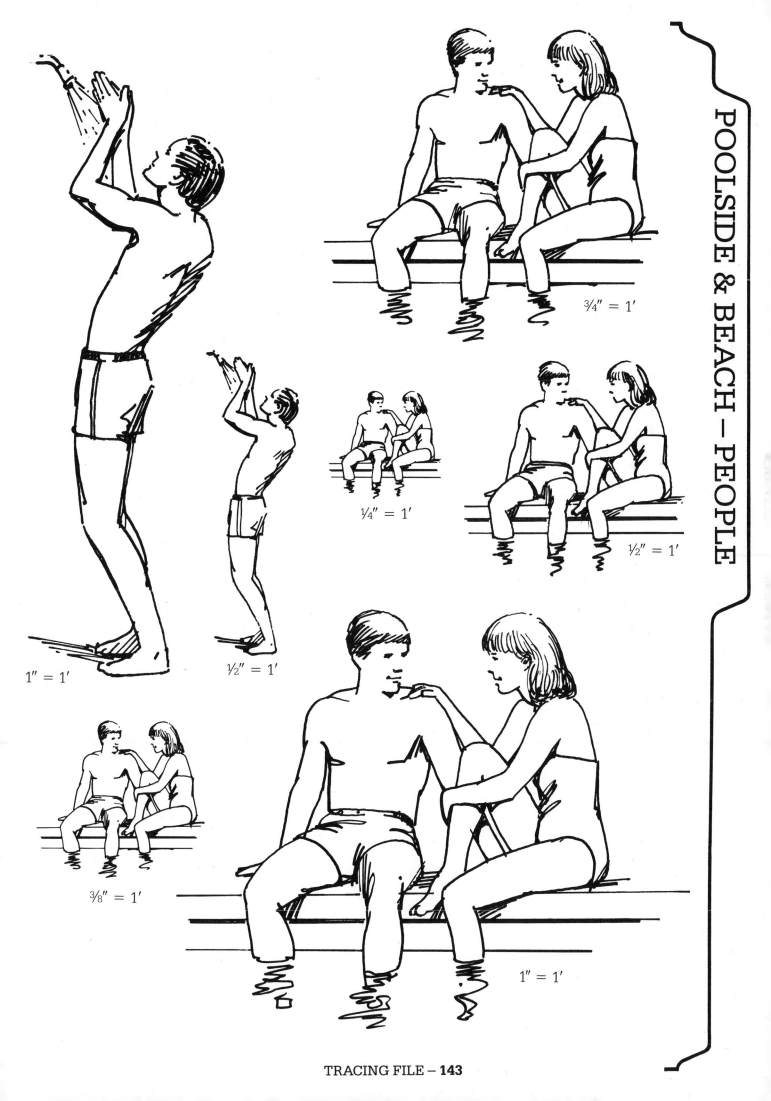

3/4" = 1'

1/4" = 1'

1/2" = 1'

1" = 1'

1/2" = 1'

3/8" = 1'

1" = 1'

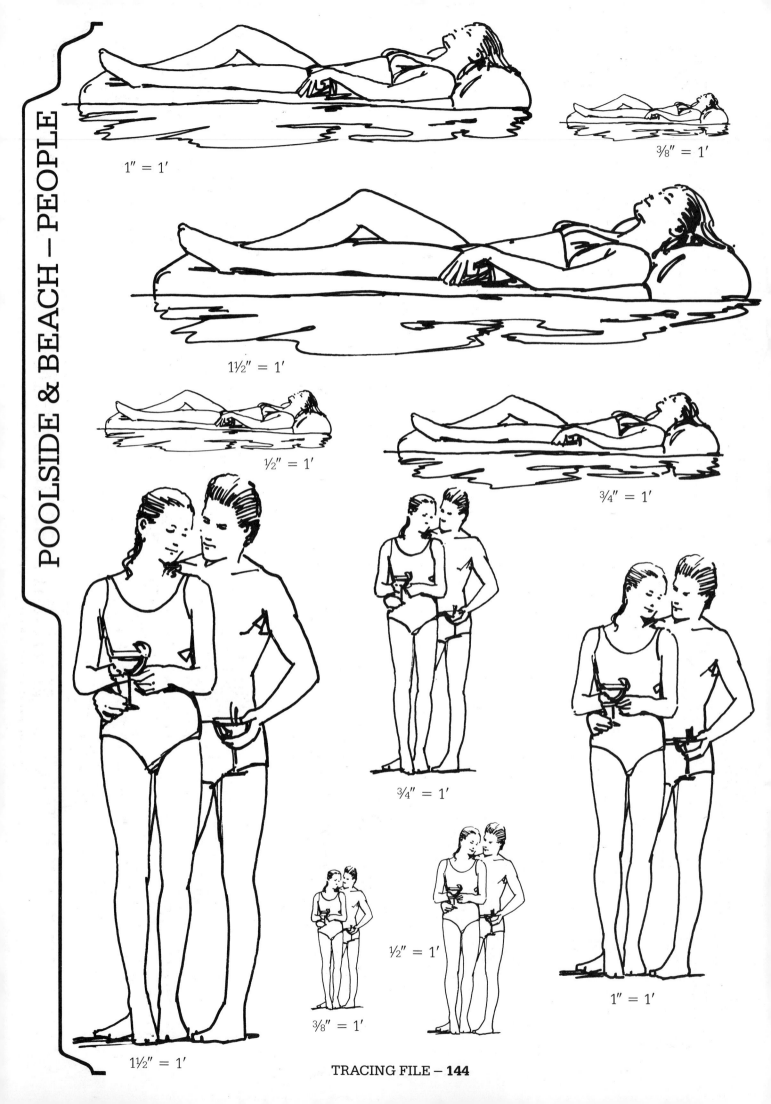

1″ = 1′

³⁄₈″ = 1′

1½″ = 1′

½″ = 1′

¾″ = 1′

¾″ = 1′

1½″ = 1′

³⁄₈″ = 1′

½″ = 1′

1″ = 1′

½″ = 1′

¾″ = 1′

¼″ = 1′

⅜″ = 1′

1″ = 1′

⅜″ = 1′

¾″ = 1′

¼″ = 1′

½″ = 1′

1″ = 1′

FOREGROUND

3/8" = 1'

1/2" = 1'

1″ = 1′

¼″ = 1′

⅜″ = 1′

¾″ = 1′

¼″ = 1′

¾″ = 1′

½″ = 1′

1″ = 1′

3/8" = 1'

1/2" = 1'

1/4" = 1'

3/8" = 1'

1" = 1'

1/2" = 1'

3/4" = 1'

3/4" = 1'

1" = 1'

3/8" = 1'

3/4" = 1'

1/2" = 1'

1" = 1'

1/4" = 1'

1/4" = 1'

3/8" = 1'

1" = 1'

1/2" = 1'

3/4" = 1'

½″ = 1′

¼″ = 1′

⅜″ = 1′

¾″ = 1′

1″ = 1′

¼″ = 1′

⅜″ = 1′

½″ = 1′

1″ = 1′

¾″ = 1′

FOREGROUND

FOREGROUND

¼″ = 1′

½″ = 1′

1″ = 1′

⅜″ = 1′

¾″ = 1′

½″ = 1′

¾″ = 1′

⅜″ = 1′

¼″ = 1′

1″ = 1′

1½″ = 1′

¼″ = 1′

⅜″ = 1′

¾″ = 1′

1″ = 1′

½″ = 1′

1½″ = 1′

½″ = 1′

¾″ = 1′

¼″ = 1′

⅜″ = 1′

⅜″ = 1′

1″ = 1′

¼″ = 1′

1″ = 1′

⅜″ = 1′

½″ = 1′

¾″ = 1′

¼″ = 1′

¾″ = 1′

1″ = 1′

⅜″ = 1′

½″ = 1′

¼" = 1'

½" = 1'

1" = 1'

⅜" = 1'

¾" = 1'

1½" = 1'

1" = 1'

3/8" = 1'

1" = 1'

1/4" = 1'

3/4" = 1'

1/2" = 1'

1/2" = 1'

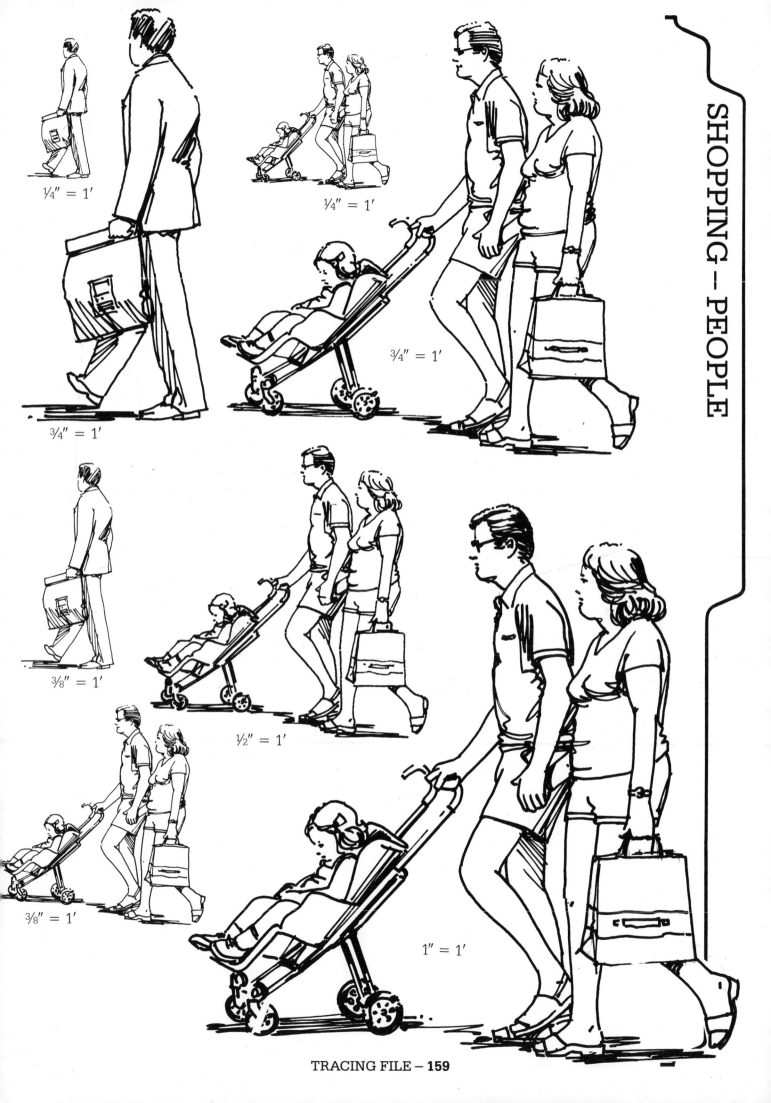

¼″ = 1′

¼″ = 1′

¾″ = 1′

¾″ = 1′

⅜″ = 1′

½″ = 1′

⅜″ = 1′

1″ = 1′

½″ = 1′

1″ = 1′

¾″ = 1′

¼″ = 1′

¾″ = 1′

⅜″ = 1′

1″ = 1′

⅜″ = 1′

½″ = 1′

¼″ = 1′

¾″ = 1′

⅜″ = 1′

½″ = 1′

½″ = 1′

¾″ = 1′

1″ = 1′

⅜″ = 1′

¼″ = 1′

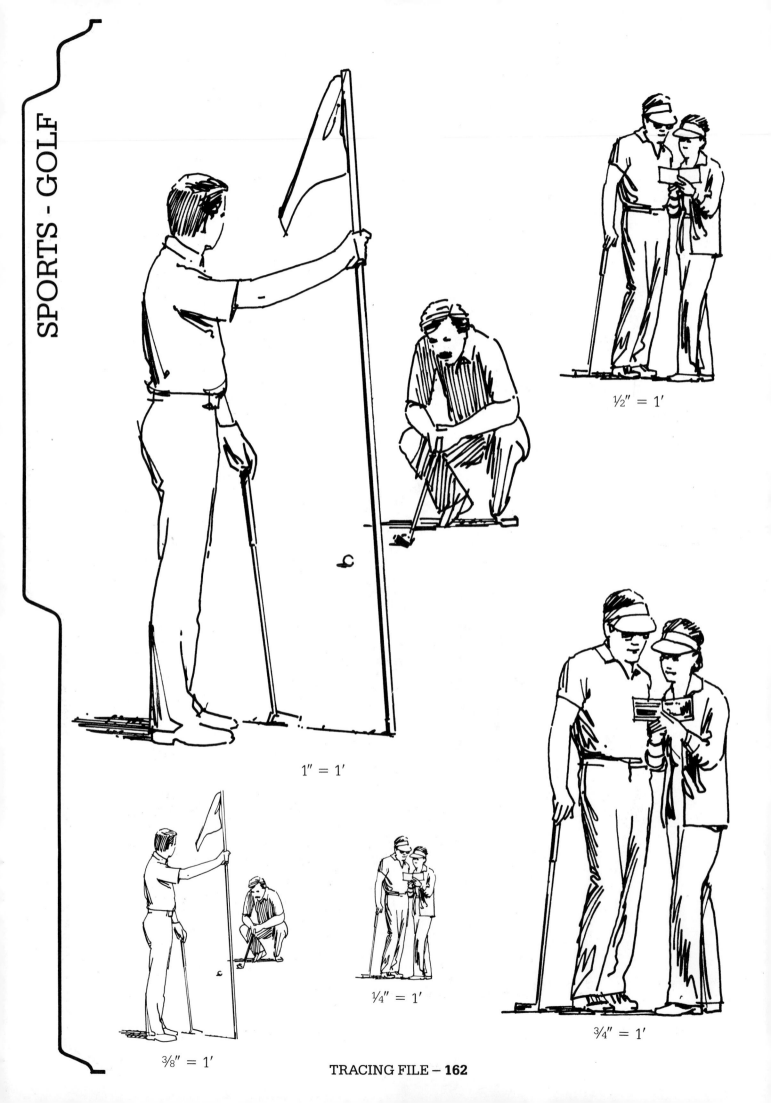

$\frac{1}{2}'' = 1'$

$1'' = 1'$

$\frac{3}{8}'' = 1'$

$\frac{1}{4}'' = 1'$

$\frac{3}{4}'' = 1'$

$\frac{3}{4}'' = 1'$

$\frac{1}{2}'' = 1'$

$\frac{3}{8}'' = 1'$

$1'' = 1'$

$\frac{3}{8}'' = 1'$

¾″ = 1′

¾″ = 1′

¼″ = 1′

⅜″ = 1′

½″ = 1′

⅜″ = 1′

¼″ = 1′

1″ = 1′

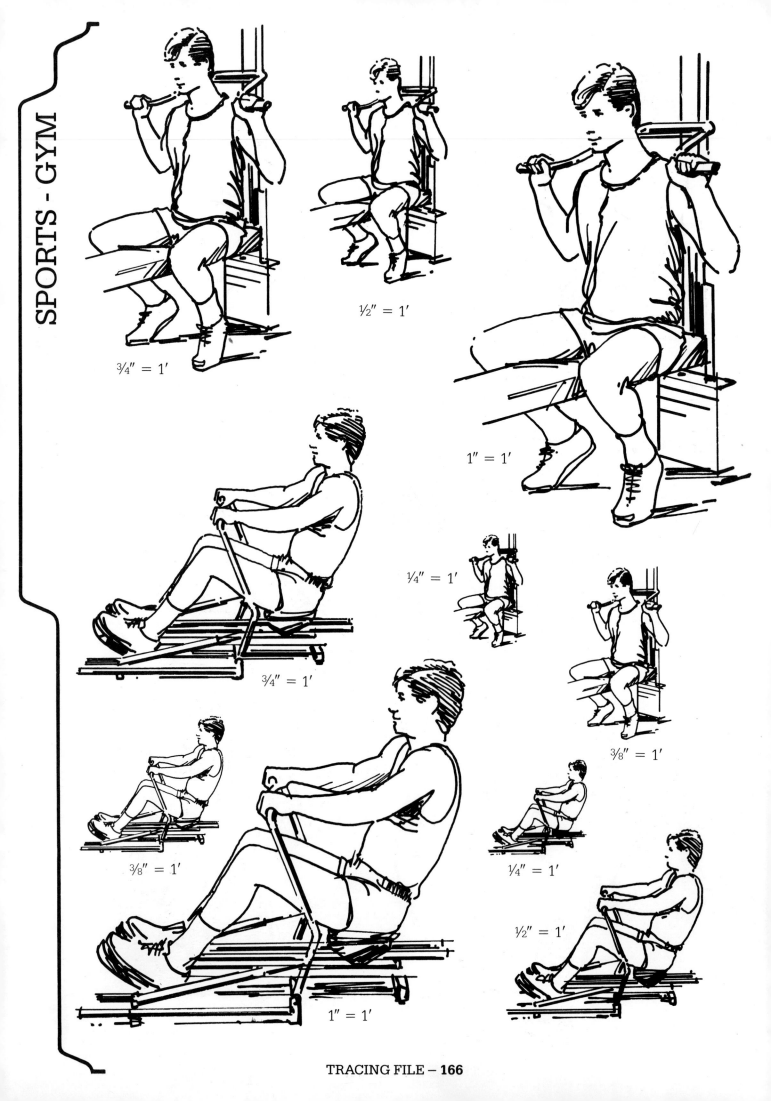

¾″ = 1′

½″ = 1′

1″ = 1′

¾″ = 1′

¼″ = 1′

⅜″ = 1′

⅜″ = 1′

1″ = 1′

¼″ = 1′

½″ = 1′

c

$\frac{3}{4}'' = 1'$

$\frac{1}{2}'' = 1'$

$\frac{1}{4}'' = 1'$

c

$\frac{3}{8}'' = 1'$

c

$1'' = 1'$

½″ = 1′

¾″ = 1′

⅜″ = 1′

¼″ = 1′

1″ = 1′

½" = 1'

½" = 1'

¼" = 1'

1" = 1'

The man throwing a football can be combined with the woman running on the opposite page to create a recreational scene.

1" = 1'

⅜" = 1'

¾" = 1'

³⁄₈″ = 1′

³⁄₄″ = 1′

¼″ = 1′

1″ = 1′

½″ = 1′

3/8" = 1'

1/4" = 1'

1" = 1'

3/4" = 1'

1/2" = 1'

3/8″ = 1′

3/4″ = 1′

1/4″ = 1′

1/2″ = 1′

1″ = 1′

3/4" = 1'

1/2" = 1'

3/8" = 1'

1/4" = 1'

1" = 1'

TRACING FILE – 173

3/8″ = 1′

1/4″ = 1′

3/4″ = 1′

1″ = 1′

1/4″ = 1′

3/4″ = 1′

1/2″ = 1′

1/2″ = 1′

1″ = 1′

3/8″ = 1′

3⁄8″ = 1′

1⁄4″ = 1′

1″ = 1′

1⁄2″ = 1′

3⁄4″ = 1′

½″ = 1′

⅜″ = 1′

1½″ = 1′

¼″ = 1′

¾″ = 1′

1″ = 1′

$\frac{1}{2}'' = 1'$

$\frac{1}{4}'' = 1'$

$1'' = 1'$

$\frac{3}{8}'' = 1'$

$\frac{3}{4}'' = 1'$

3/4" = 1'

1/2" = 1'

1/4" = 1'

3/8" = 1'

1" = 1'

½″ = 1′

1″ = 1′

¾″ = 1′

¼″ = 1′

⅜″ = 1′

1″ = 1′

½″ = 1′

¼″ = 1′

⅜″ = 1′

¾″ = 1′

3/4″ = 1′

1/2″ = 1′

3/8″ = 1′

1/4″ = 1′

1″ = 1′

¾″ = 1′

⅜″ = 1′

1″ = 1′

½″ = 1′

¼″ = 1′

3/8" = 1'

1/4" = 1'

1" = 1'

1/2" = 1'

3/4" = 1'

1½" = 1'

TELEPHONE – PEOPLE

also see page 130

1″ = 1′

½″ = 1′

⅜″ = 1′

1½″ = 1′

¼″ = 1′

¾″ = 1′

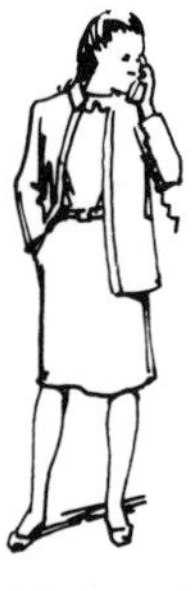

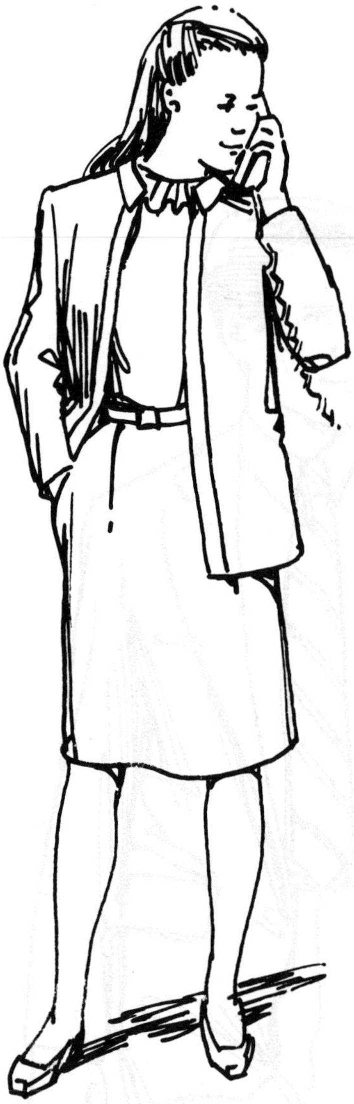

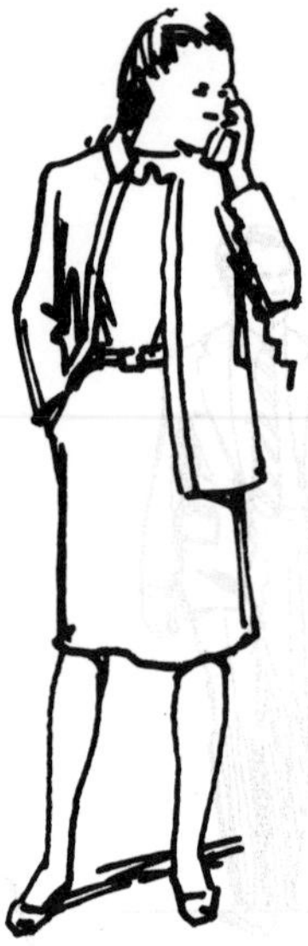

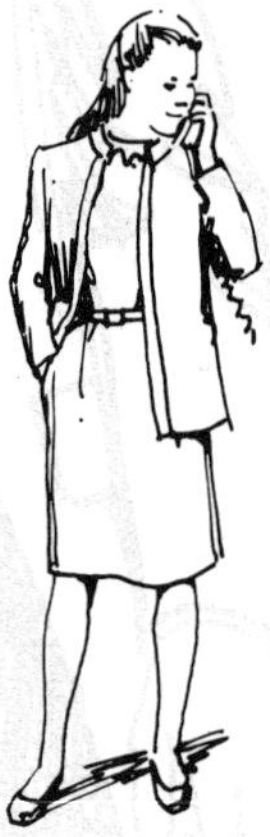

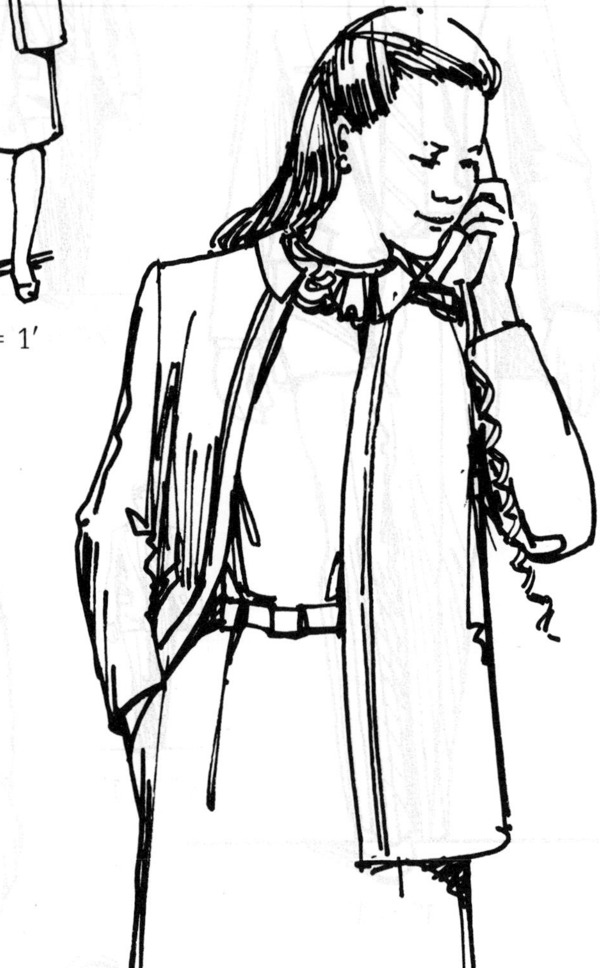

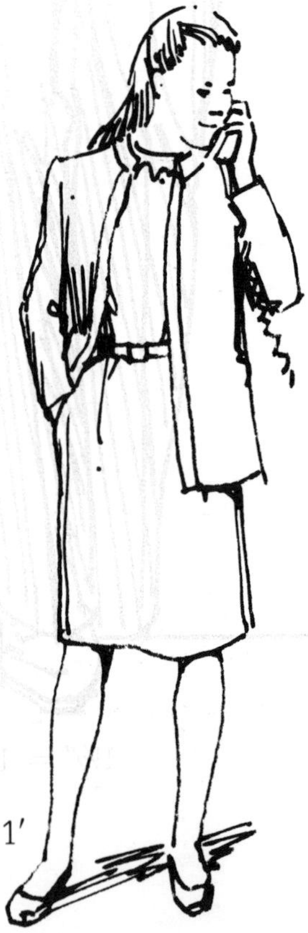

½″ = 1′

1″ = 1′

¼″ = 1′

⅜″ = 1′

¾″ = 1′

1½″ = 1′

$1'' = 1'$

$\frac{3}{4}'' = 1'$

$\frac{1}{2}'' = 1'$

$1\frac{1}{2}'' = 1'$

FOREGROUND

¼″ = 1′

⅜″ = 1′

¾″ = 1′

½″ = 1′

1″ = 1′

1½″ = 1′

29″

¾″ = 1′

⅜″ = 1′

½″ = 1′

1″ = 1′

¼″ = 1′

¾″ = 1′

1″ = 1′

¼″ = 1′

⅜″ = 1′

½″ = 1′

WOMEN – LEANING

1″ = 1′

½″ = 1′

¾″ = 1′

¼″ = 1′

⅜″ = 1′

½″ = 1′

¾″ = 1′

1″ = 1′

¼″ = 1′

⅜″ = 1′

$3/8'' = 1'$

$1/4'' = 1'$

$1'' = 1'$

$3/4'' = 1'$

$1/2'' = 1'$

$1\frac{1}{2}'' = 1'$

$3/8'' = 1'$

$1/2'' = 1'$

$1'' = 1'$

$3/4'' = 1'$

$1'' = 1'$

$1/4'' = 1'$

$3/8'' = 1'$

¼″ = 1′

½″ = 1′

¾″ = 1′

1″ = 1′

¾″ = 1′

⅜″ = 1′

¼″ = 1′

½″ = 1′

WOMEN – SITTING

also see pages 84 and 85

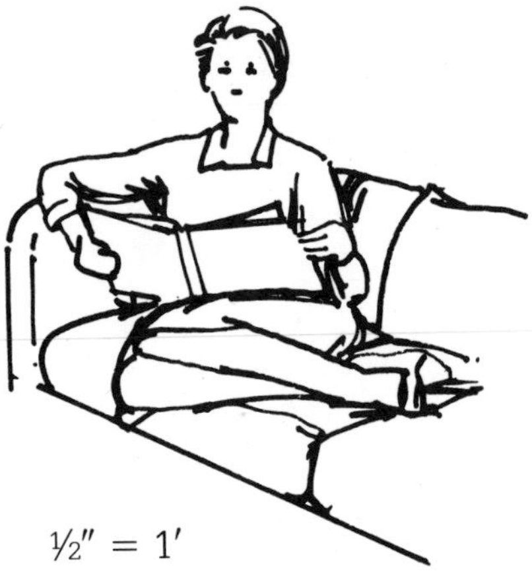

½″ = 1′

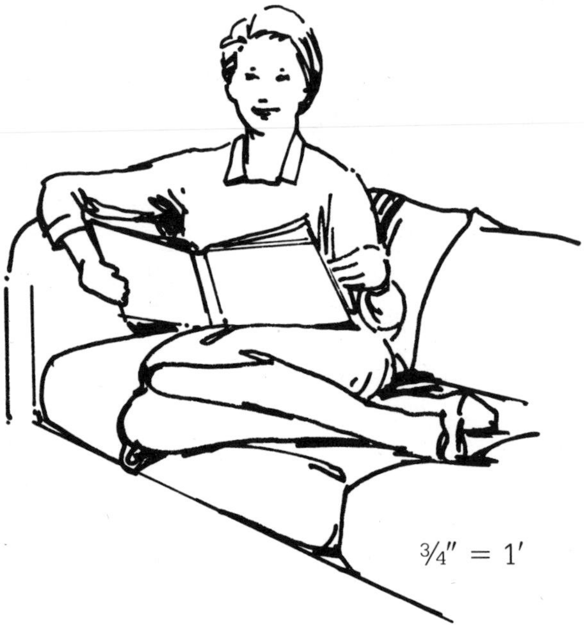

¾″ = 1′

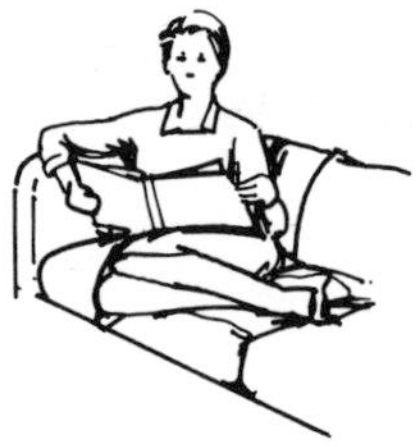

¼″ = 1′

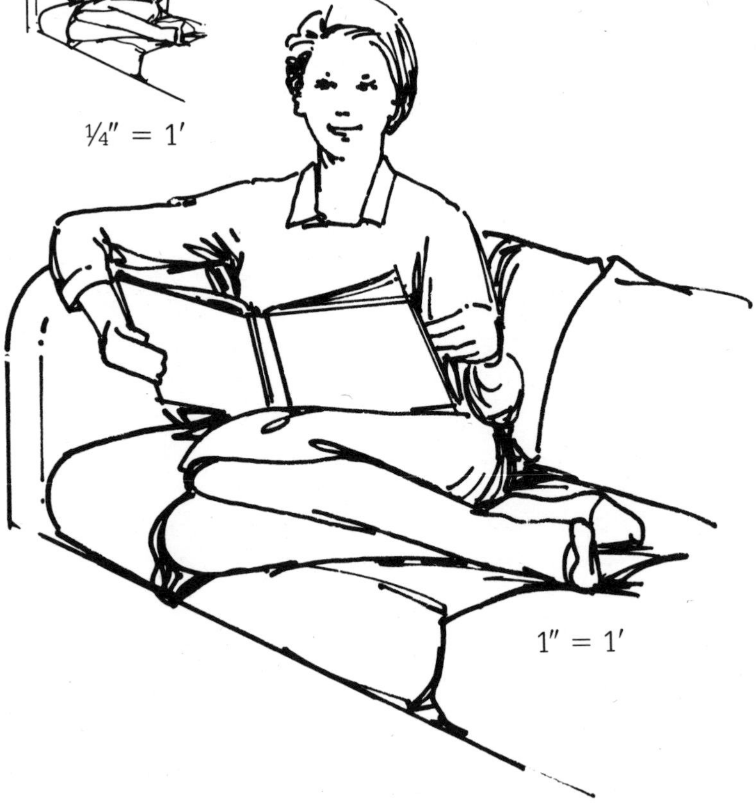

1″ = 1′

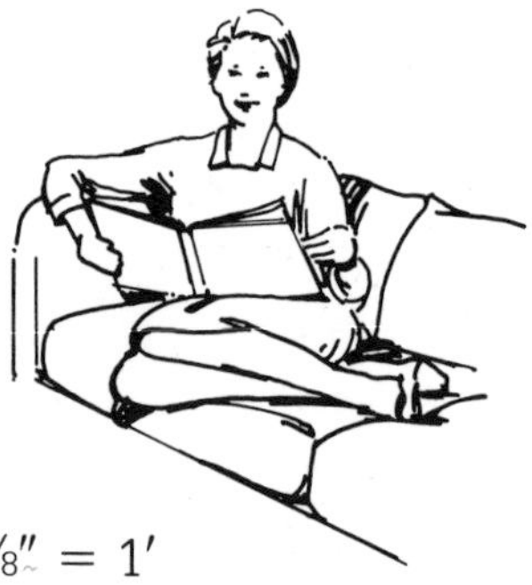

⅜″ = 1′

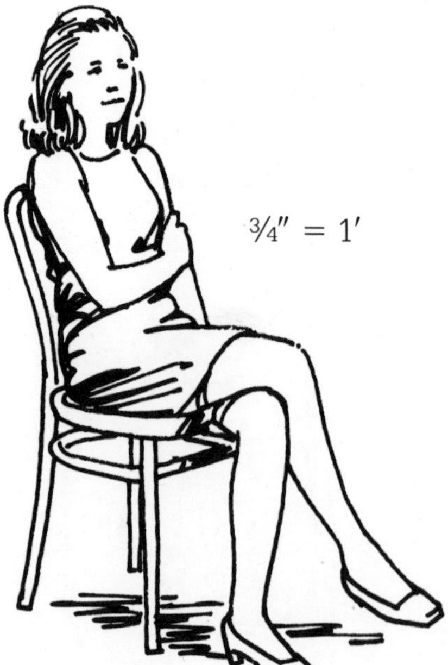

¾″ = 1′

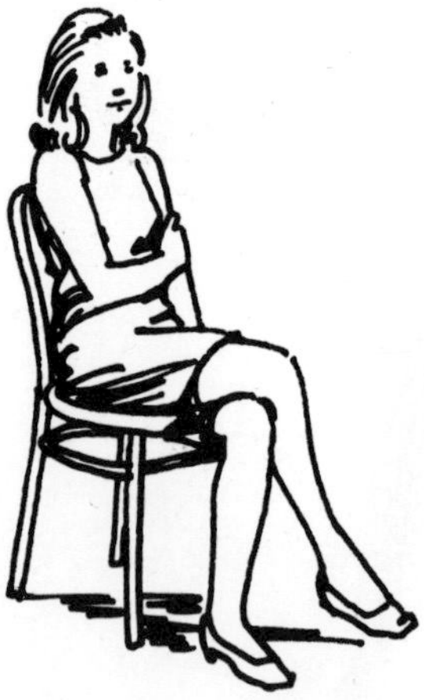

½″ = 1′

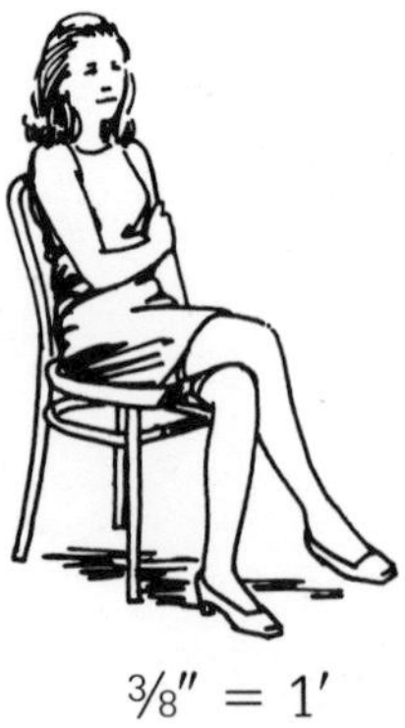

⅜″ = 1′

3⁄8″ = 1′

½″ = 1′

1″ = 1′

¼″ = 1′

3⁄4″ = 1′

1″ = 1′

¼″ = 1′

¼″ = 1′

3/8″ = 1′

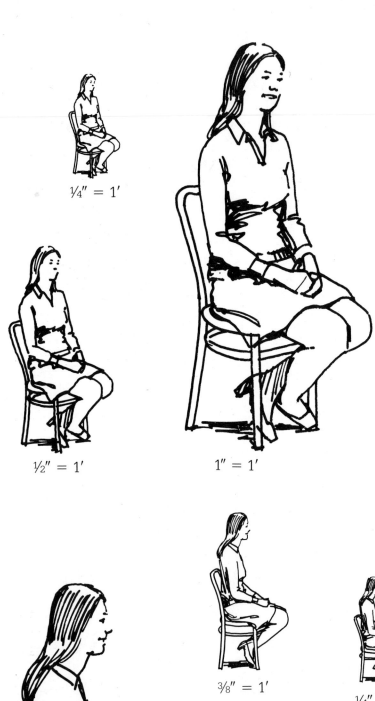

½″ = 1′

1″ = 1′

3/4″ = 1′

3/8″ = 1′

¼″ = 1′

1″ = 1′

½″ = 1′

3/4″ = 1′

3/8″ = 1′

1/4″ = 1′

3/4″ = 1′

1″ = 1′

1/4″ = 1′

1/2″ = 1′

1/2″ = 1′

3/4″ = 1′

3/8″ = 1′

1″ = 1′

$\frac{1}{2}'' = 1'$

$\frac{1}{4}'' = 1'$

$\frac{3}{4}'' = 1'$

$1'' = 1'$

FOREGROUND

$\frac{3}{8}'' = 1'$

1" = 1'

½" = 1'

¼" = 1'

1½" = 1'

⅜" = 1'

¾" = 1'

WOMEN – STANDING

¾″ = 1′

½″ = 1′

¼″ = 1′

⅜″ = 1′

1″ = 1′

1½″ = 1′

⅜″ = 1′

¾″ = 1′

1″ = 1′

¼″ = 1′

½″ = 1′

½″ = 1′

1″ = 1′

¼″ = 1′

1½″ = 1′

⅜″ = 1′

¾″ = 1′

$\frac{3}{8}'' = 1'$

$\frac{1}{4}'' = 1'$

$\frac{3}{4}'' = 1'$

$1'' = 1'$

$1'' = 1'$

FOREGROUND

$\frac{1}{4}'' = 1'$

$\frac{1}{2}'' = 1'$

3/8" = 1'

1/2" = 1'

3/4" = 1'

1/2" = 1'

1 1/2" = 1'

1" = 1'

3/4" = 1'

3/8" = 1'

1/4" = 1'

1″ = 1′

½″ = 1′

⅜″ = 1′

¼″ = 1′

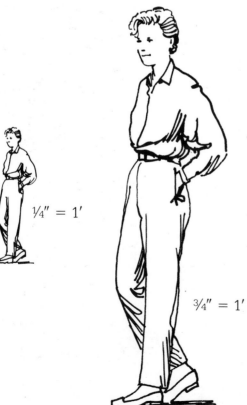

¾″ = 1′

1½″ = 1′

¼″ = 1′

¾″ = 1′

½″ = 1′

⅜″ = 1′

⅜″ = 1′

¼″ = 1′

1″ = 1′

½″ = 1′

¾″ = 1′

1″ = 1′

3/8" = 1'

1/4" = 1'

1" = 1'

FOREGROUND

1/2" = 1'

3/4" = 1'

¼″ = 1′

⅜″ = 1′

½″ = 1′

¾″ = 1′

½″ = 1′

1″ = 1′

¼″ = 1′

⅜″ = 1′

1″ = 1′

¾″ = 1′

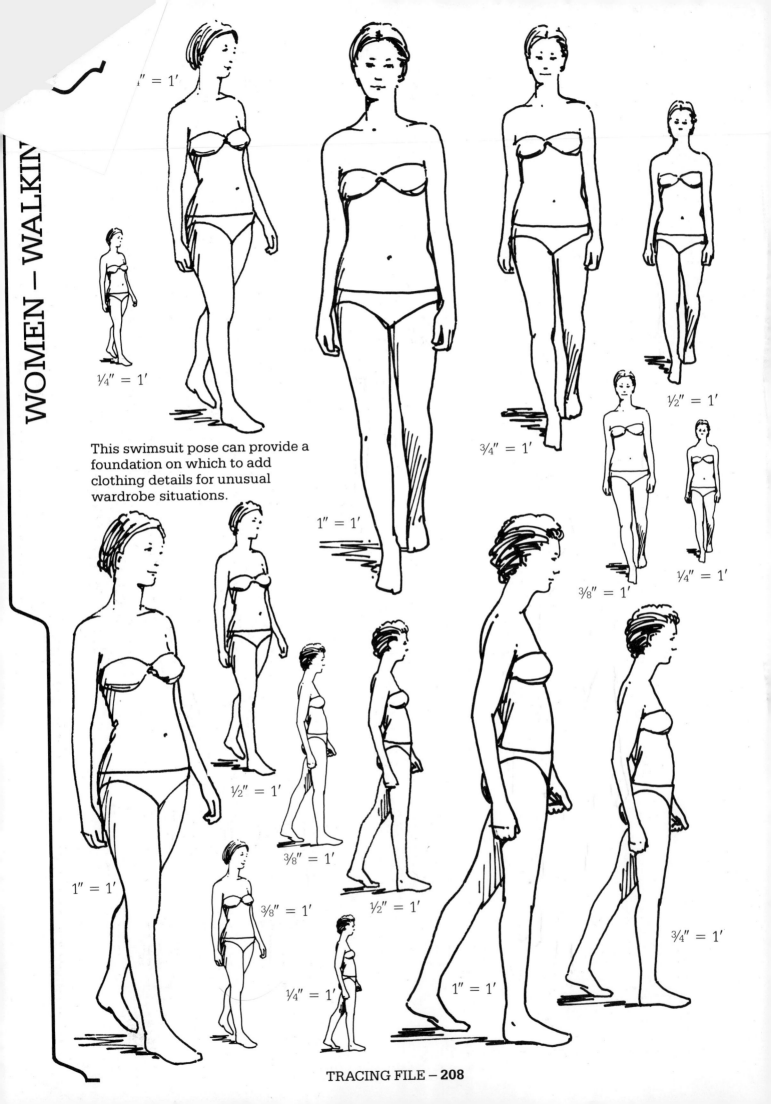

1″ = 1′

¼″ = 1′

This swimsuit pose can provide a
foundation on which to add
clothing details for unusual
wardrobe situations.

¾″ = 1′

1″ = 1′

½″ = 1′

¼″ = 1′

⅜″ = 1′

½″ = 1′

⅜″ = 1′

1″ = 1′

⅜″ = 1′

½″ = 1′

¼″ = 1′

1″ = 1′

¾″ = 1′

TRACING FILE – 208

¼" = 1'

½" = 1'

¾" = 1'

1" = 1'

⅜" = 1'

1½" = 1'

⅜" = 1'

1" = 1'

¾" = 1'

½" = 1'

¼" = 1'

INTERIOR FOLIAGE

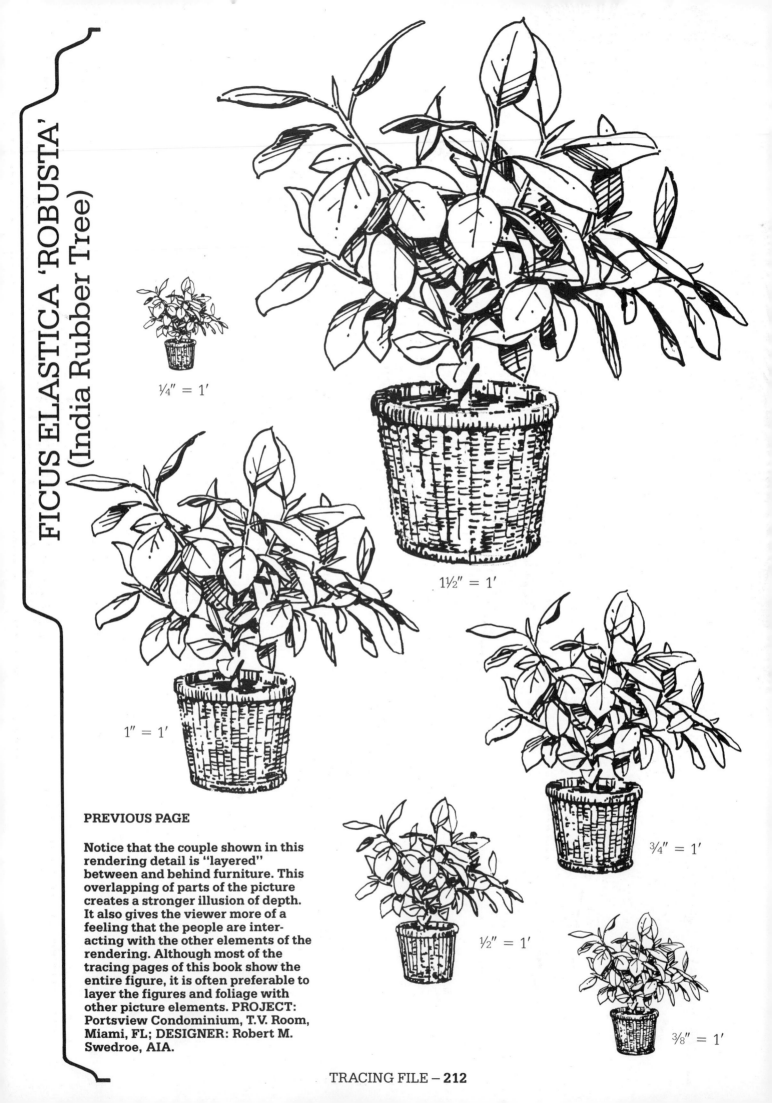

FICUS ELASTICA 'ROBUSTA' (India Rubber Tree)

¼" = 1'

1½" = 1'

1" = 1'

PREVIOUS PAGE

Notice that the couple shown in this rendering detail is "layered" between and behind furniture. This overlapping of parts of the picture creates a stronger illusion of depth. It also gives the viewer more of a feeling that the people are interacting with the other elements of the rendering. Although most of the tracing pages of this book show the entire figure, it is often preferable to layer the figures and foliage with other picture elements. PROJECT: Portsview Condominium, T.V. Room, Miami, FL; DESIGNER: Robert M. Swedroe, AIA.

½" = 1'

¾" = 1'

⅜" = 1'

CHRYSALIDOCARPUS LUTESCENS
(Areca Palm)

FOREGROUND

CHRYSALIDOCARPUS LUTESCENS
(Areca Palm)

¼″ = 1′

⅜″ = 1′

1″ = 1′

½″ = 1′

¾″ = 1′

CHRYSALIDOCARPUS LUTESCENS
(Areca Palm)

$1\frac{1}{2}'' = 1'$

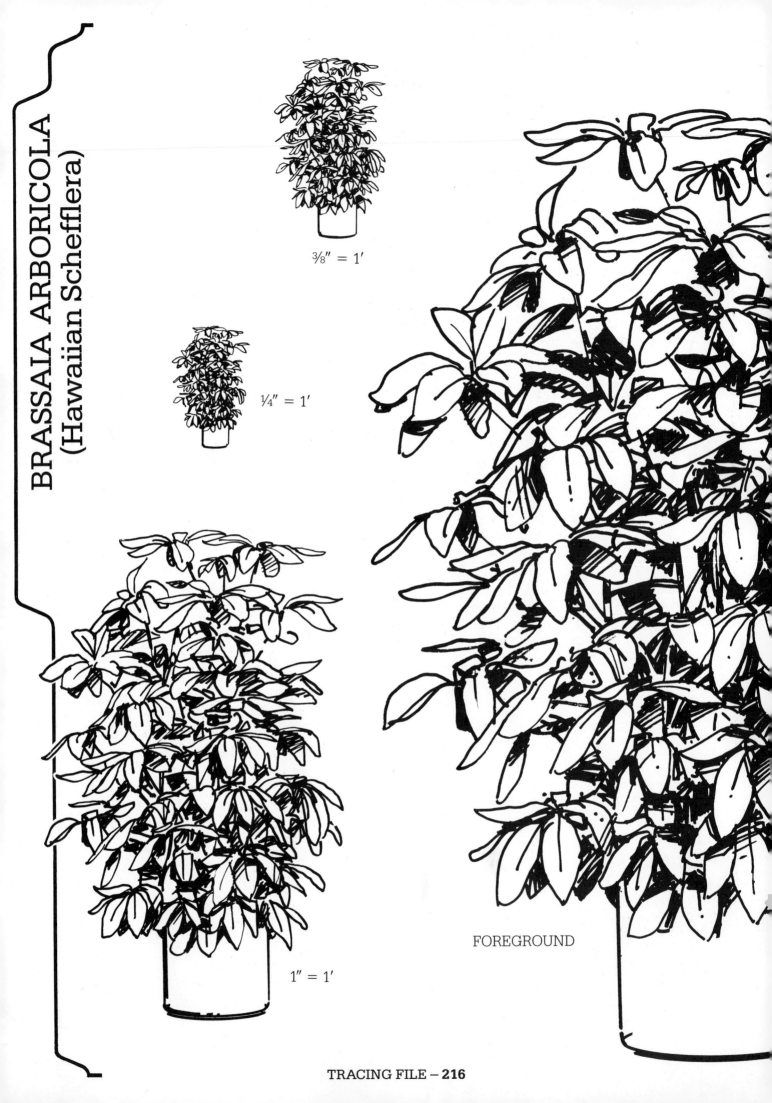

BRASSAIA ARBORICOLA
(Hawaiian Schefflera)

$3/8'' = 1'$

$1/4'' = 1'$

$1'' = 1'$

FOREGROUND

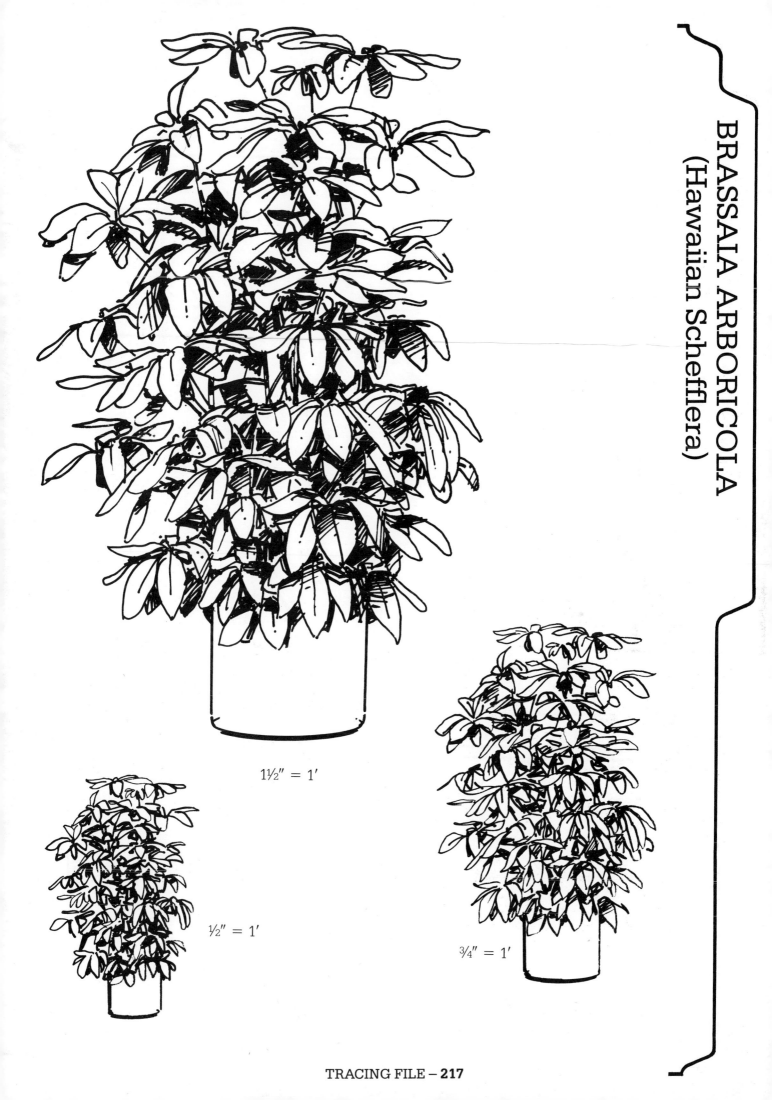

BRASSAIA ARBORICOLA
(Hawaiian Schefflera)

$1\frac{1}{2}'' = 1'$

$\frac{1}{2}'' = 1'$

$\frac{3}{4}'' = 1'$

BRASSAIA ACTINOPHYLLA
(Schefflera)

1½″ = 1′

3/8″ = 1′

1/2″ = 1′

FOREGROUND

BRASSAIA ACTINOPHYLLA
(Schefflera)

$\frac{3}{4}'' = 1'$

$\frac{1}{4}'' = 1'$

$1'' = 1'$

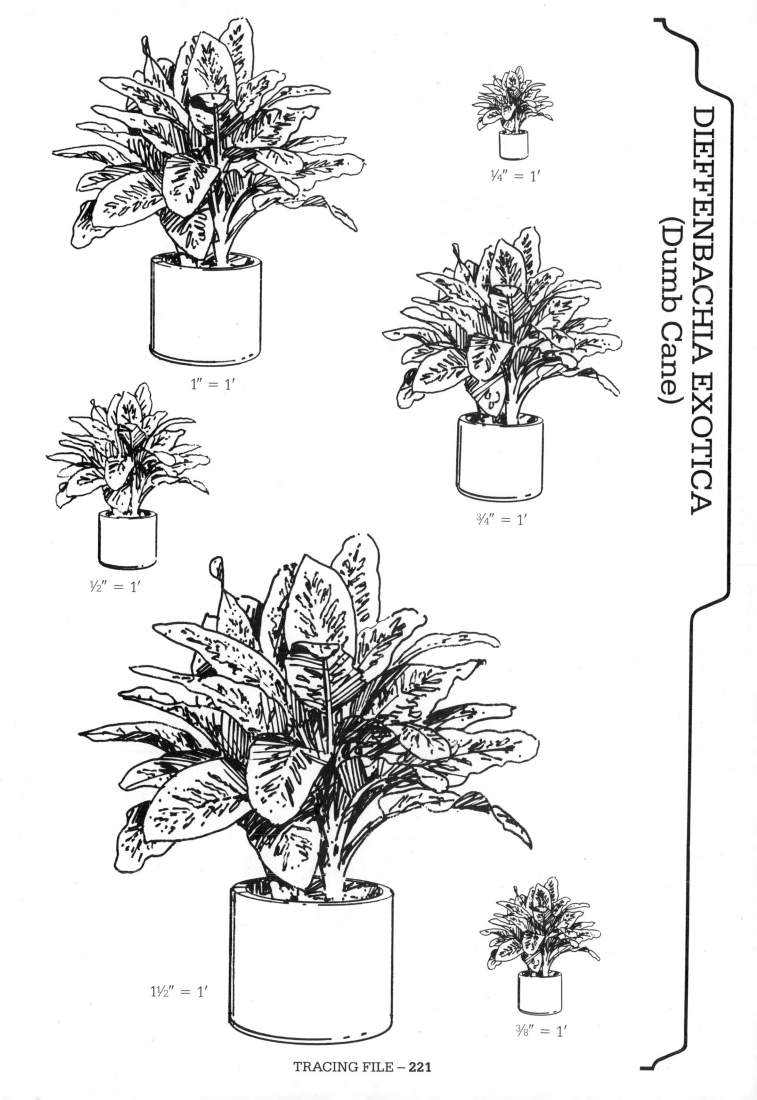

¼″ = 1′

1″ = 1′

¾″ = 1′

½″ = 1′

1½″ = 1′

⅜″ = 1′

CYCAS REVOLUTA
(Sago Palm)

¼″ = 1′

½″ = 1′

1½″ = 1′

¾″ = 1′

CYCAS REVOLUTA
(Sago Palm)

$\frac{3}{8}'' = 1'$

FOREGROUND

$1'' = 1'$

DRACAENA MASSANGEANA
(Corn Plant)

3/8" = 1'

1/4" = 1'

1" = 1'

FOREGROUND

DRACAENA MASSANGEANA
(Corn Plant)

½″ = 1′

1½″ = 1′

¾″ = 1′

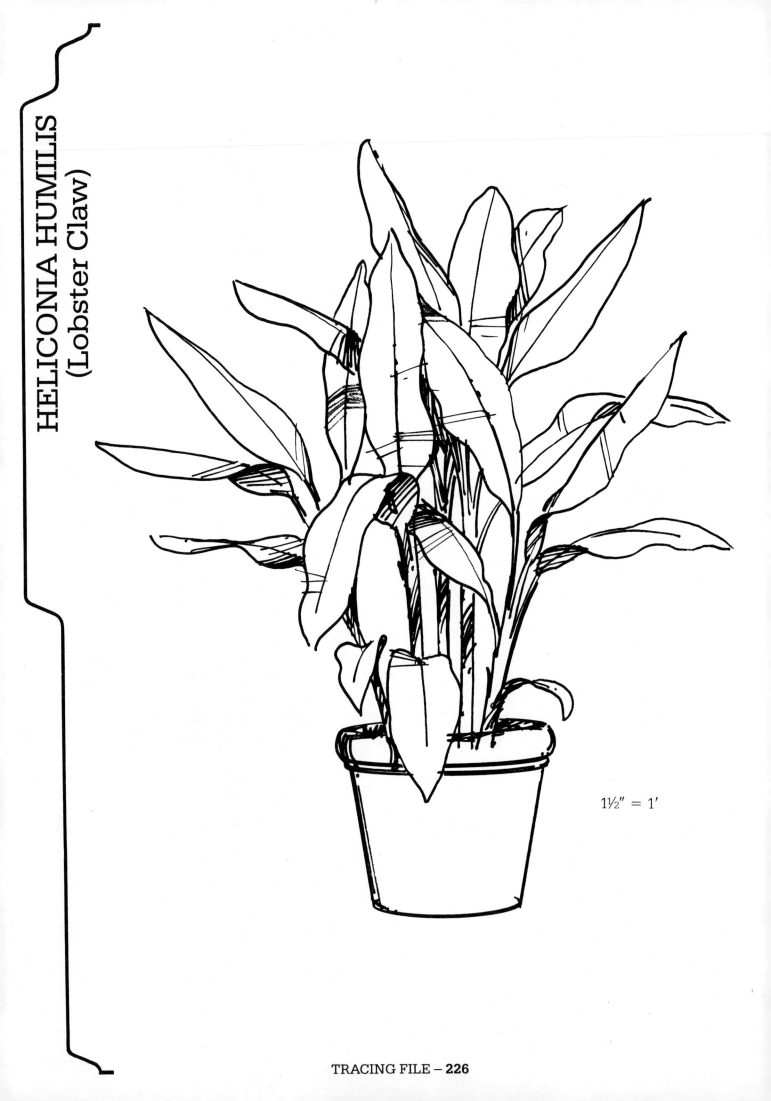

HELICONIA HUMILIS
(Lobster Claw)

1½″ = 1′

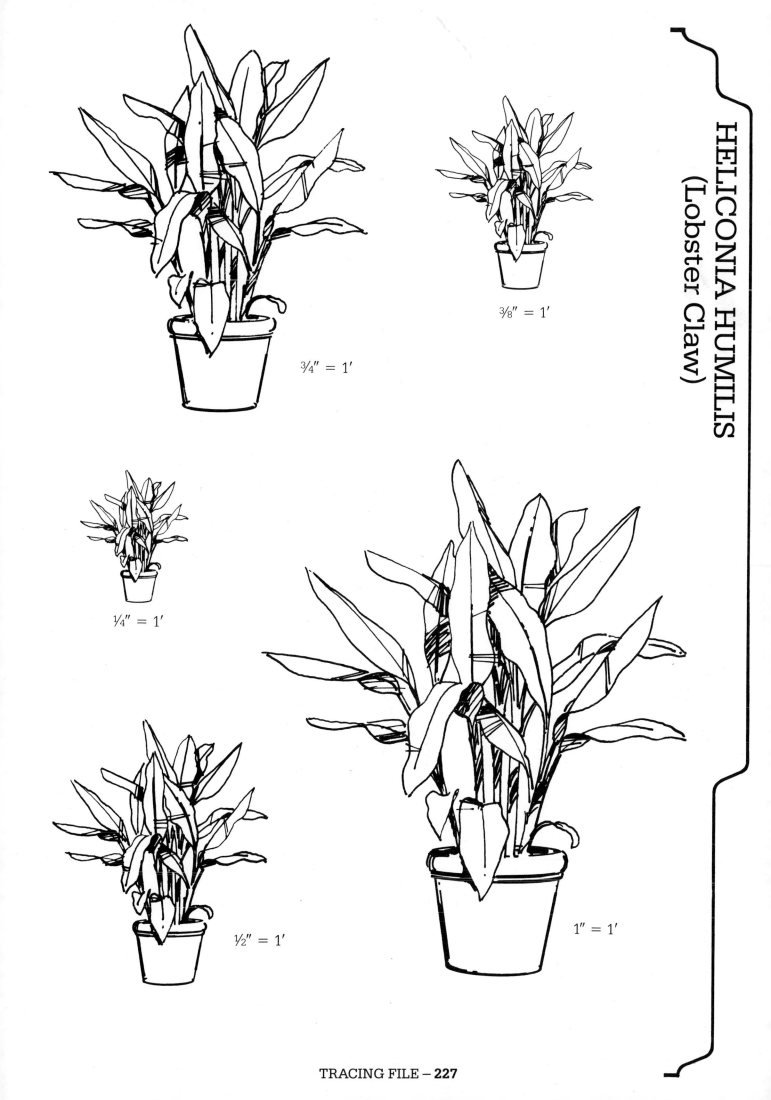

$\frac{3}{8}'' = 1'$

$\frac{3}{4}'' = 1'$

$\frac{1}{4}'' = 1'$

$\frac{1}{2}'' = 1'$

$1'' = 1'$

BEAUCARNEA RECURVATA
(Pony Tail)

1½″ = 1′

⅜″ = 1′

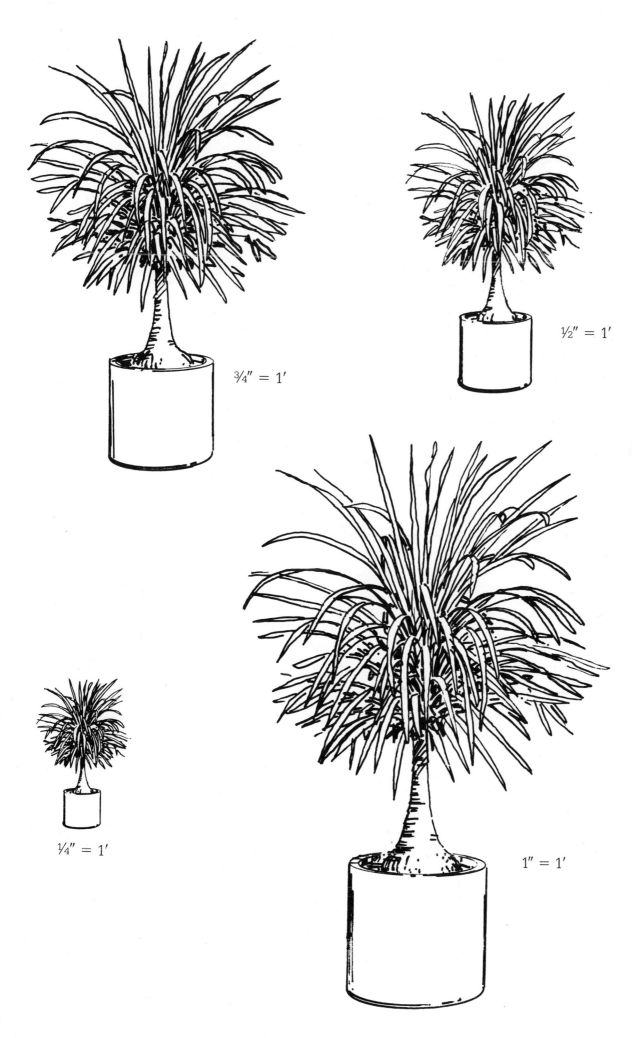

¾″ = 1′

½″ = 1′

¼″ = 1′

1″ = 1′

PANDANUS UTILIS
(Screw Pine)

$1\frac{1}{2}'' = 1'$

$\frac{1}{2}'' = 1'$

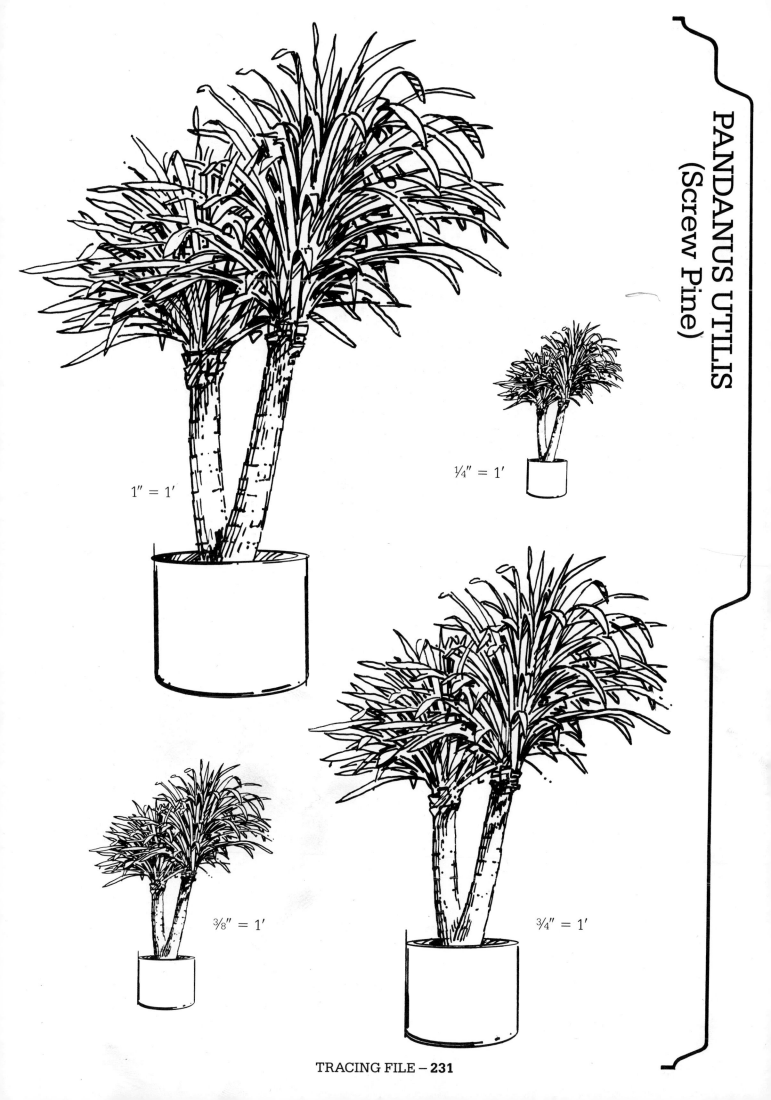

PANDANUS UTILIS
(Screw Pine)

1″ = 1′

¼″ = 1′

⅜″ = 1′

¾″ = 1′

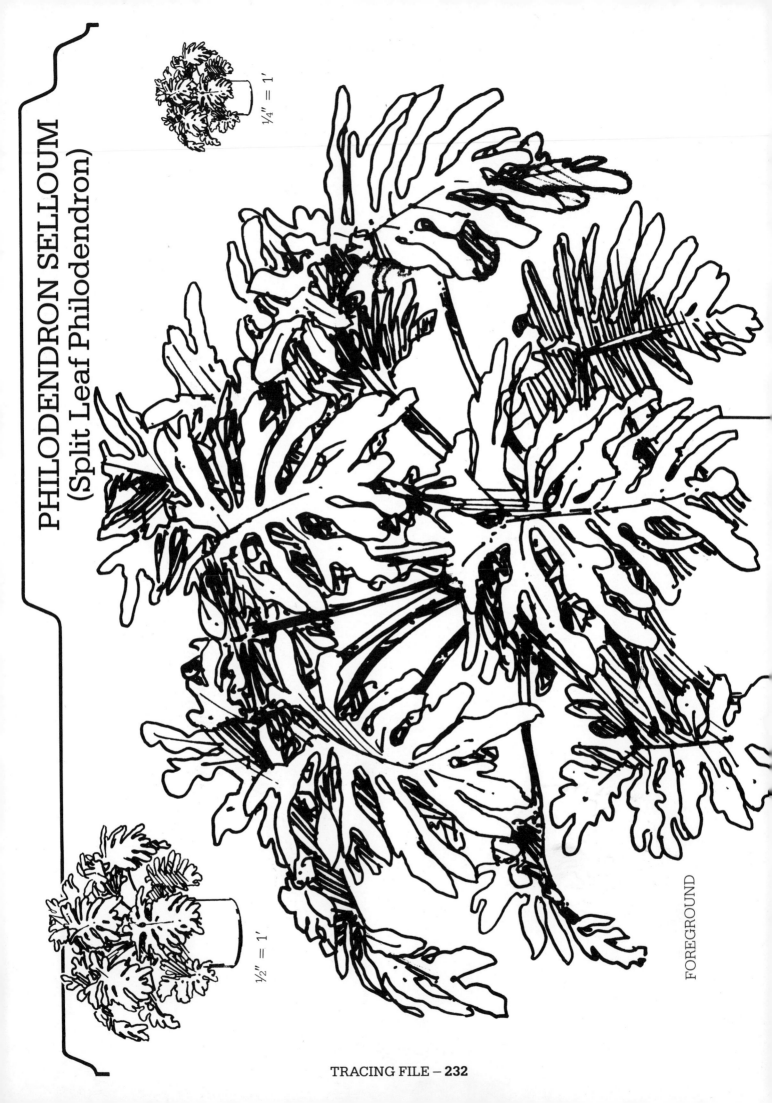

PHILODENDRON SELLOUM
(Split Leaf Philodendron)

¼" = 1'

½" = 1'

FOREGROUND

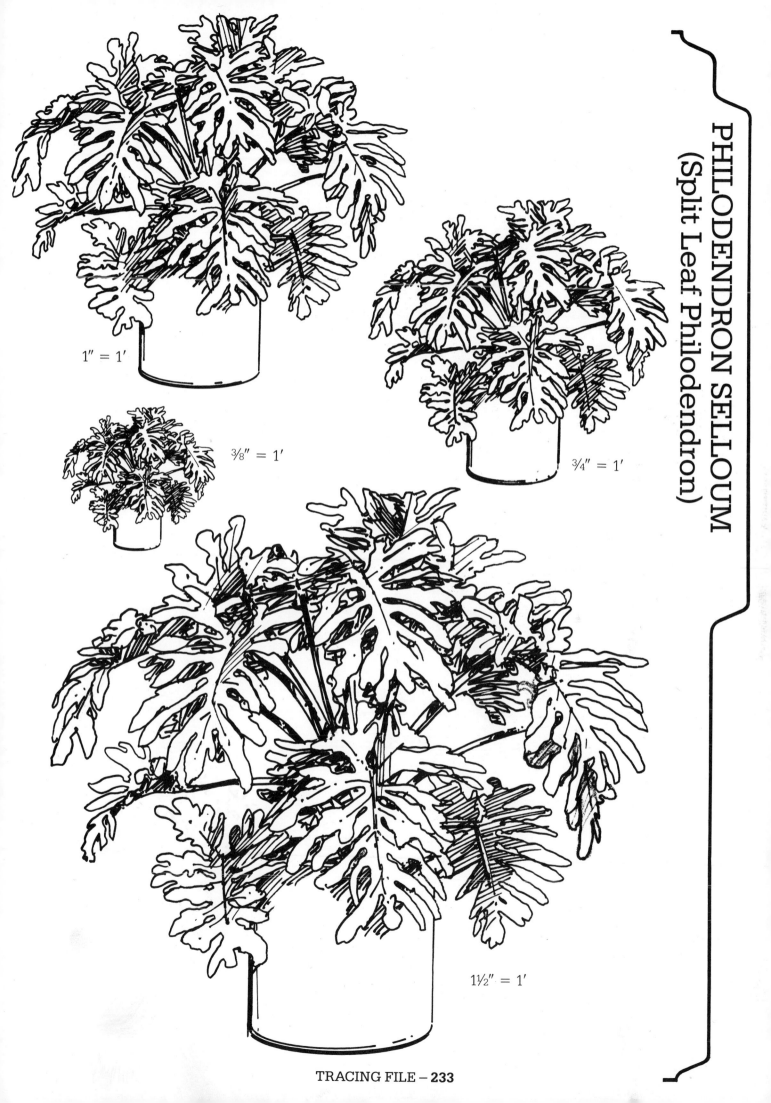

1″ = 1′

3/8″ = 1′

3/4″ = 1′

1½″ = 1′

RHAPIS EXCELSA
(Lady Palm)

¼″ = 1′

⅜″ = 1′

1½″ = 1′

¾″ = 1′

RHAPIS EXCELSA
(Lady Palm)

½″ = 1′

FOREGROUND

1″ = 1′

YUCCA ELEPHANTIPES
(Spineless Yucca)

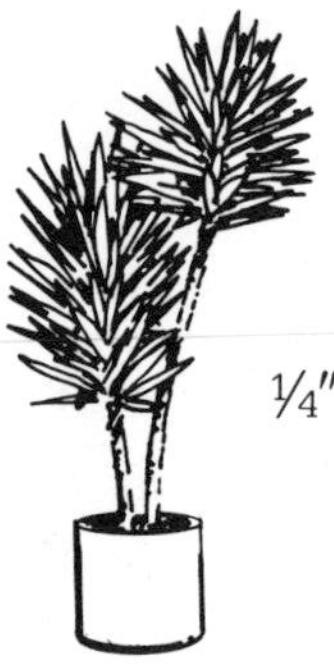

¼″ = 1′

½″ = 1′

1½″ = 1′

¾″ = 1′

⅜″ = 1′

FOREGROUND

1″ = 1′

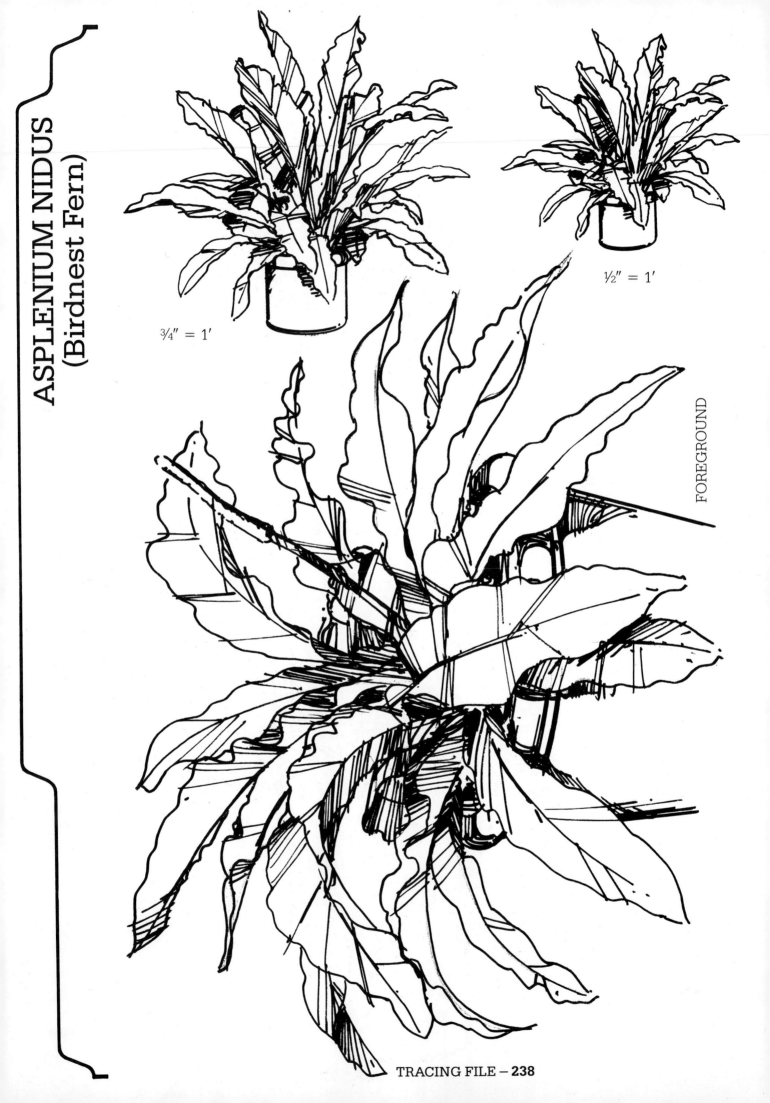

ASPLENIUM NIDUS
(Birdnest Fern)

¾″ = 1′

½″ = 1′

FOREGROUND

TRACING FILE – 238

ASPLENIUM NIDUS
(Birdnest Fern)

¼″ = 1′

⅜″ = 1′

1″ = 1′

1½″ = 1′

STRELITZIA NICOLAI
(White Bird of Paradise)

3⁄8″ = 1′

1⁄2″ = 1′

1″ = 1′

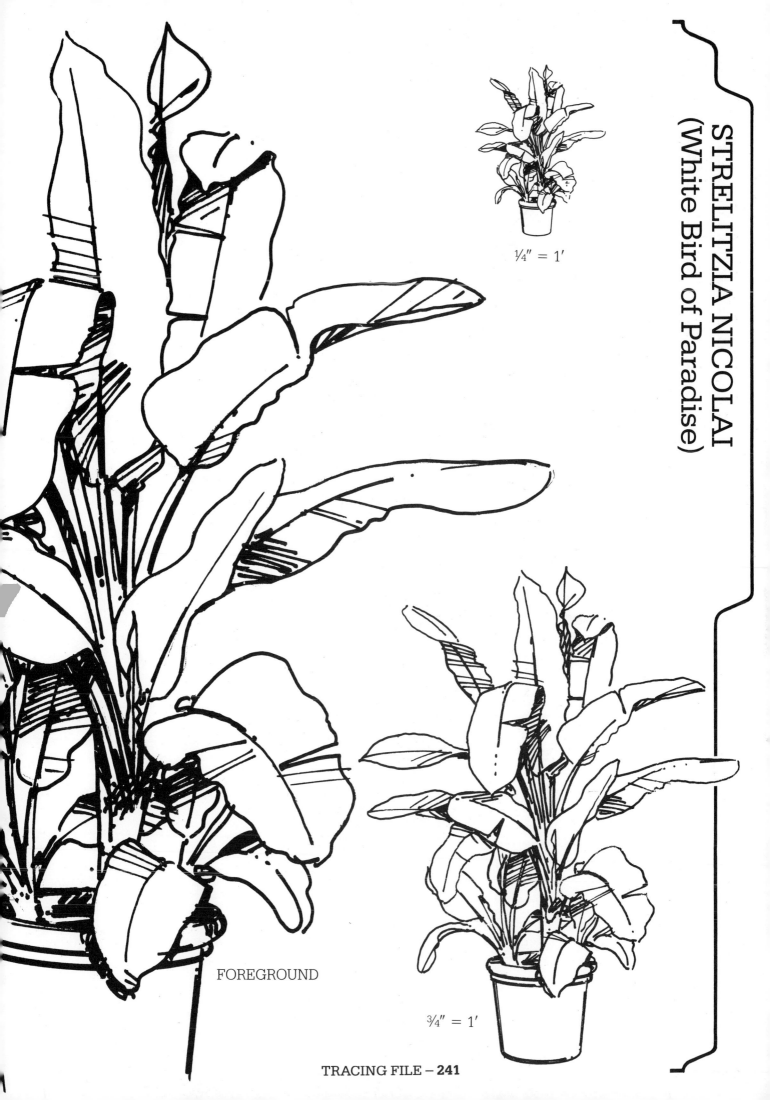

¼″ = 1′

FOREGROUND

¾″ = 1′

STRELITZIA NICOLAI
(White Bird of Paradise)

1½" = 1'

$\frac{1}{4}'' = 1'$

$\frac{1}{2}'' = 1'$

HOWEIA FORSTERIANA
(Kentia Palm)

FOREGROUND

$\frac{3}{8}'' = 1'$

HOWEIA FORSTERIANA
(Kentia Palm)

1½" = 1'

$\frac{3}{4}'' = 1'$

$1'' = 1'$

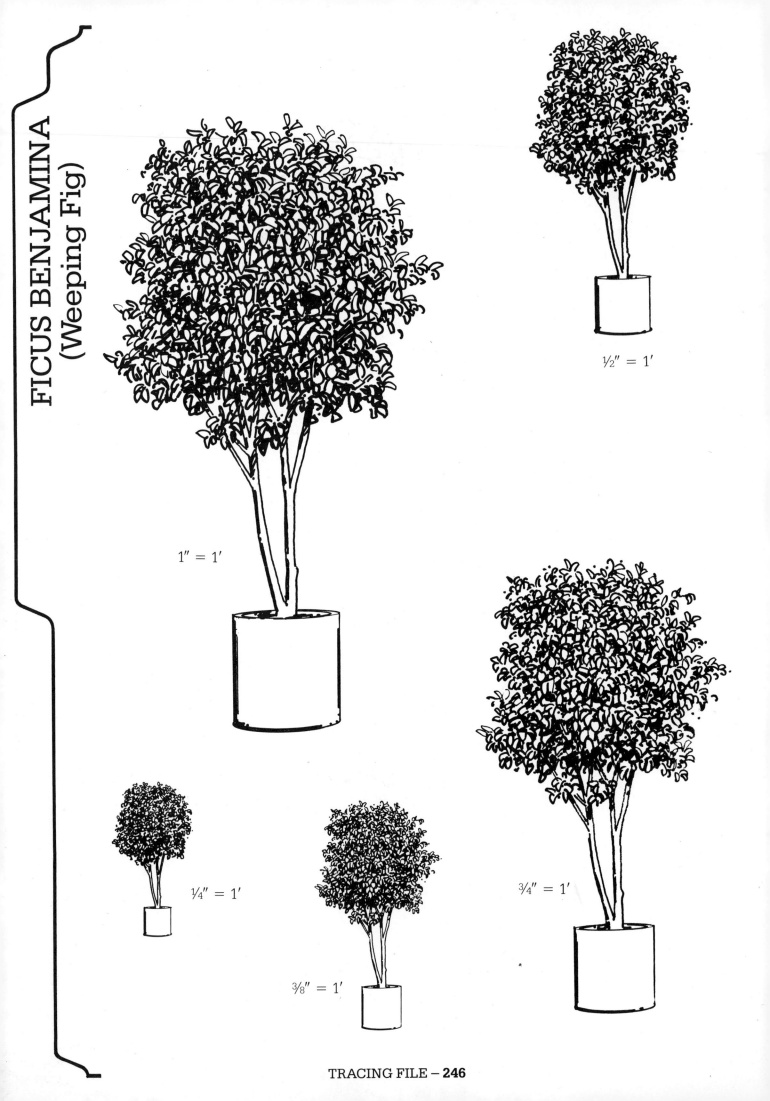

FICUS BENJAMINA (Weeping Fig)

½″ = 1′

1″ = 1′

¾″ = 1′

¼″ = 1′

⅜″ = 1′

$1\frac{1}{2}'' = 1'$

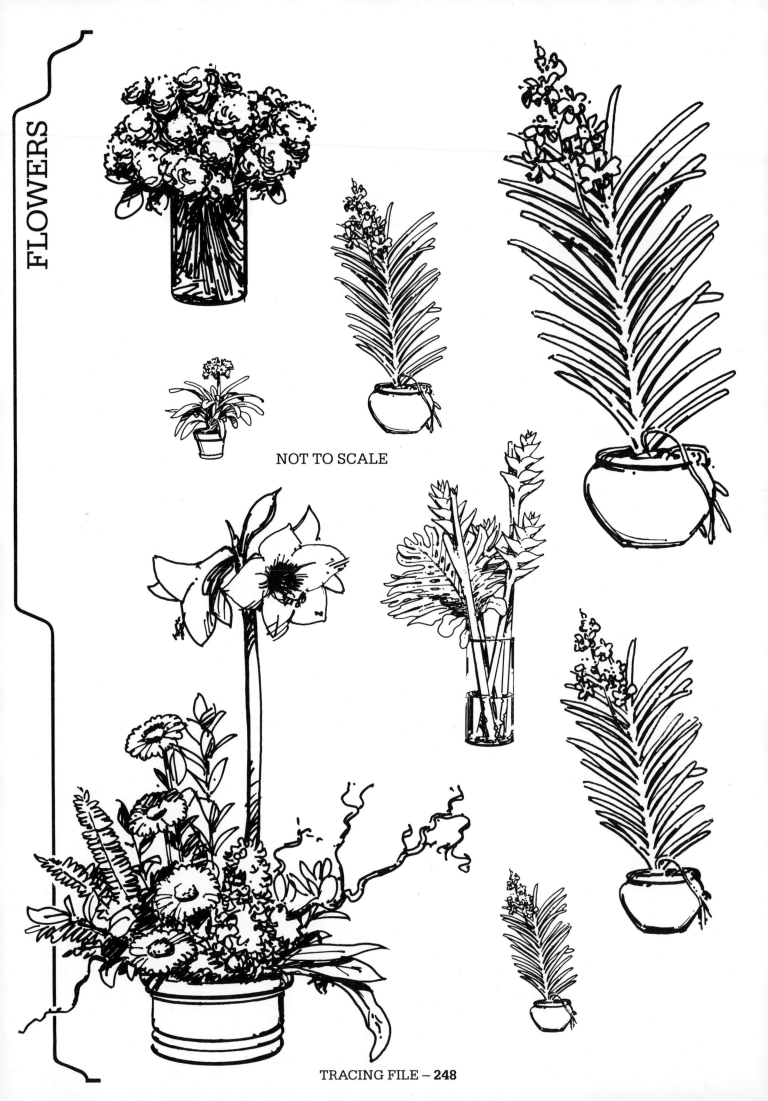

NOT TO SCALE

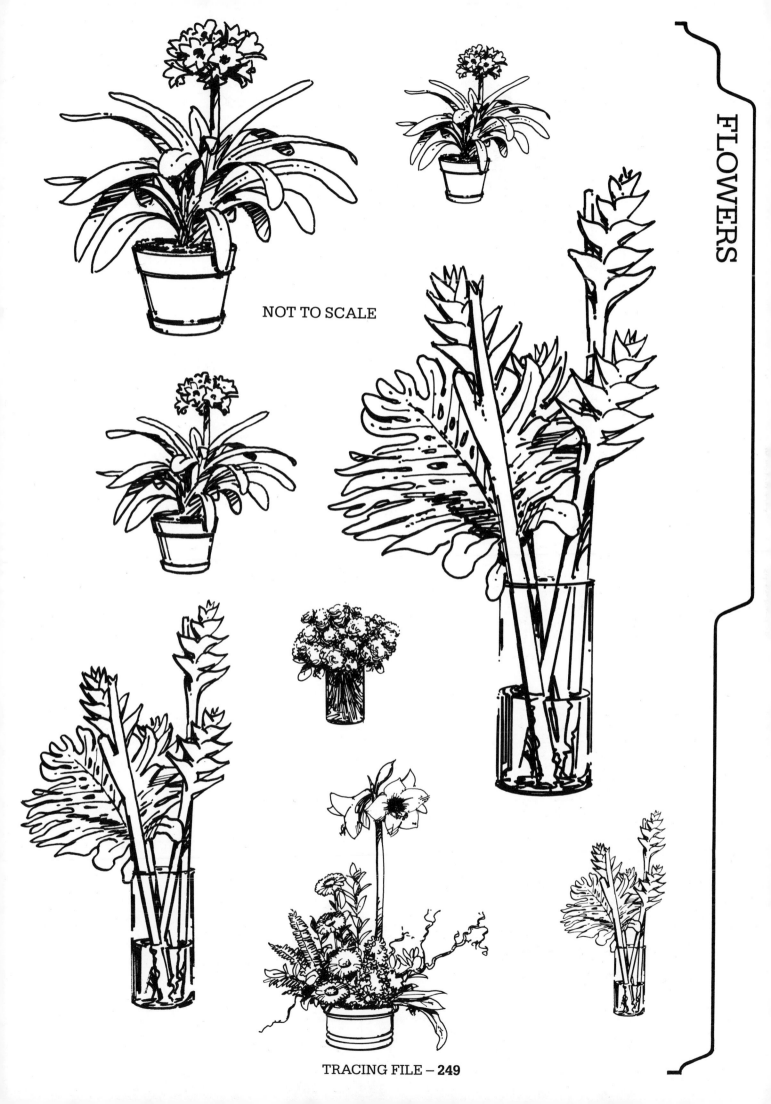

NOT TO SCALE

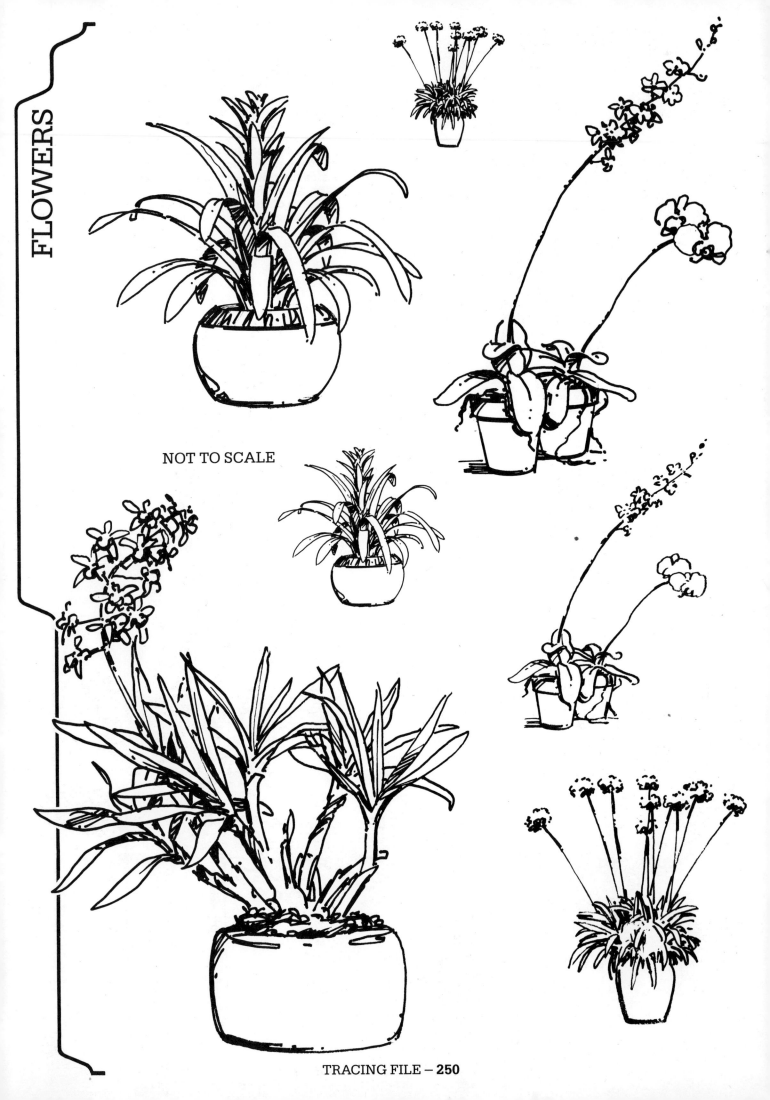

FLOWERS

NOT TO SCALE

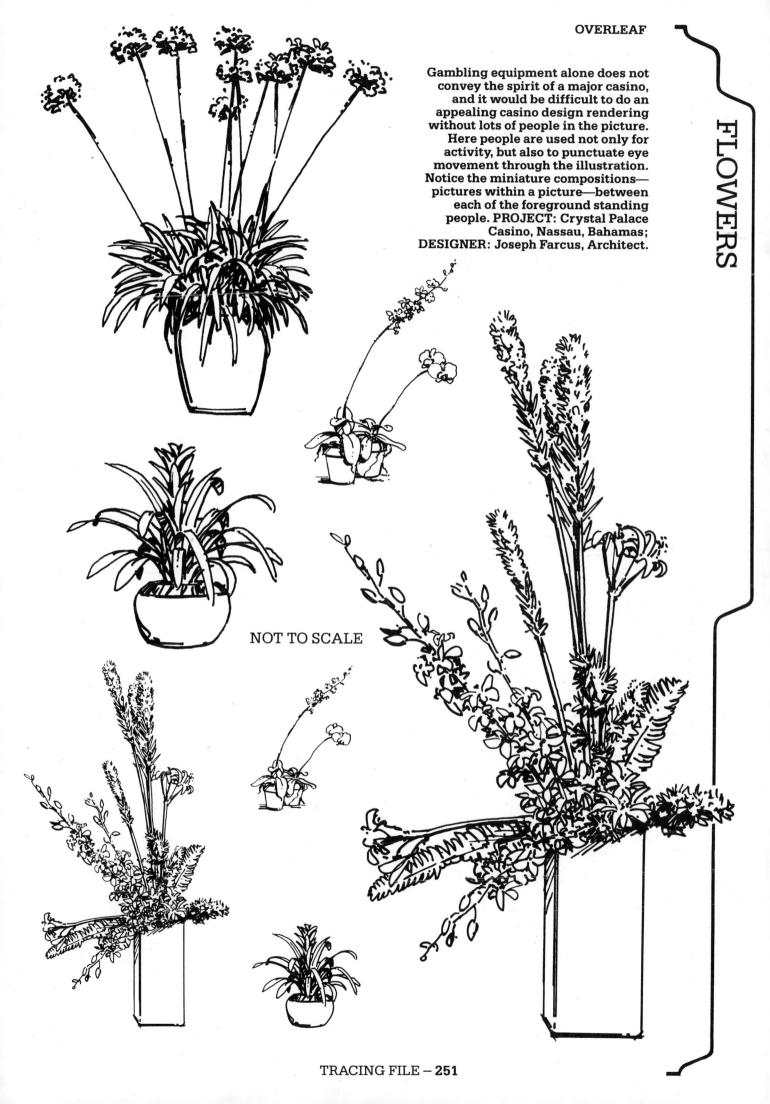

Gambling equipment alone does not convey the spirit of a major casino, and it would be difficult to do an appealing casino design rendering without lots of people in the picture. Here people are used not only for activity, but also to punctuate eye movement through the illustration. Notice the miniature compositions—pictures within a picture—between each of the foreground standing people. PROJECT: Crystal Palace Casino, Nassau, Bahamas; DESIGNER: Joseph Farcus, Architect.

FLOWERS

NOT TO SCALE

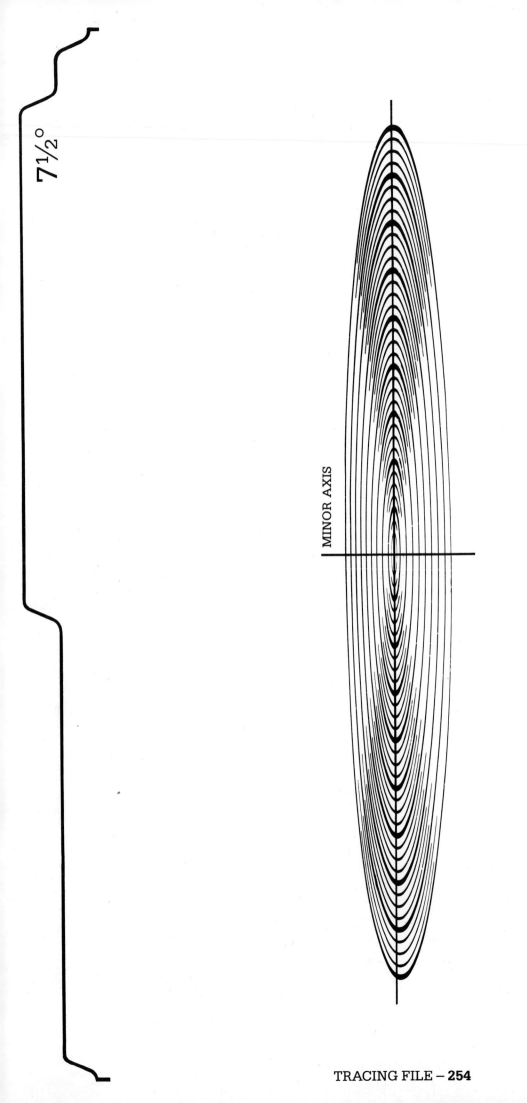

$7\frac{1}{2}°$

MINOR AXIS

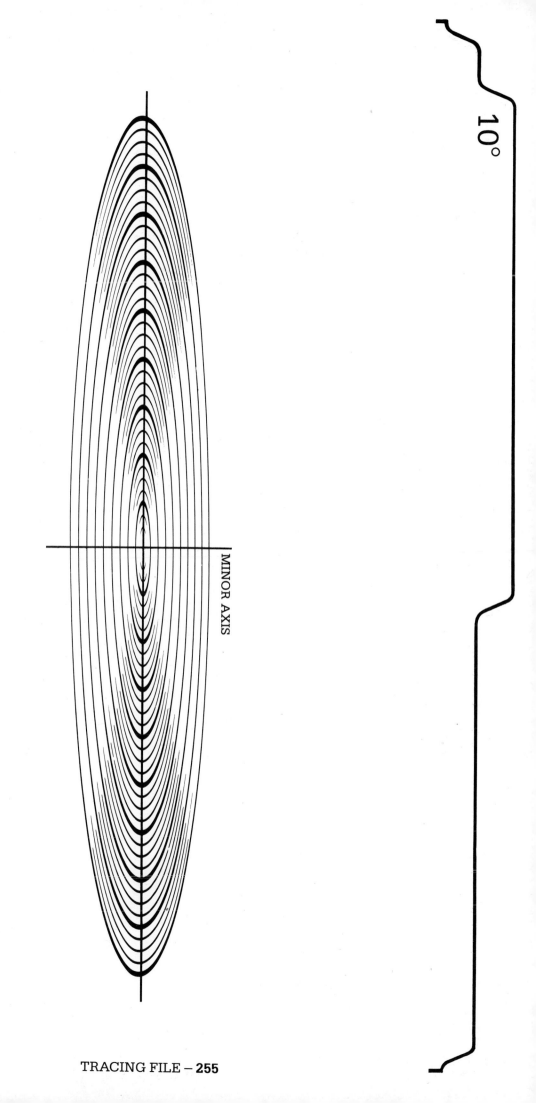

MINOR AXIS

10°

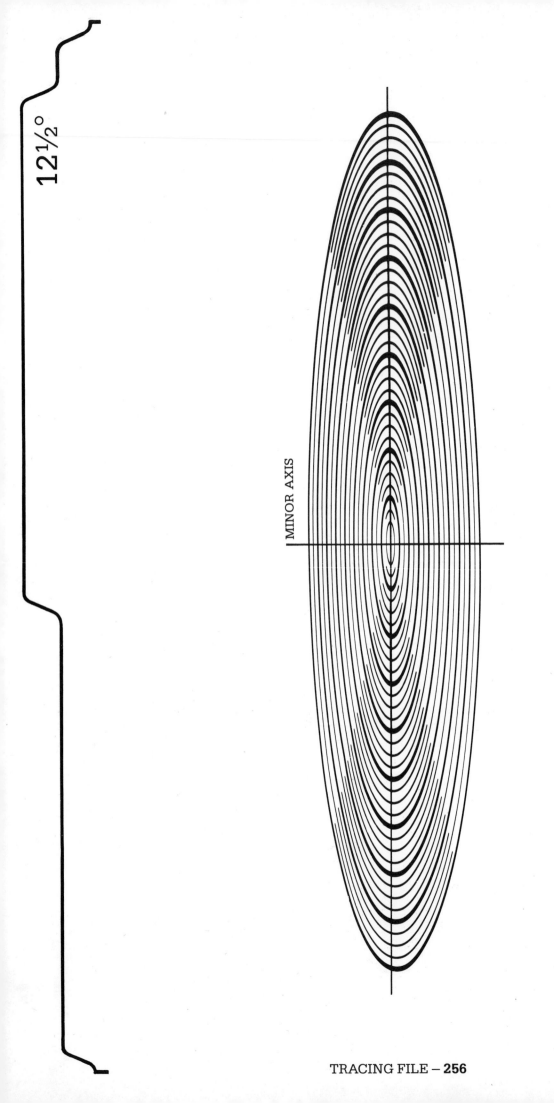

MINOR AXIS

$12\frac{1}{2}°$

TRACING FILE – **256**

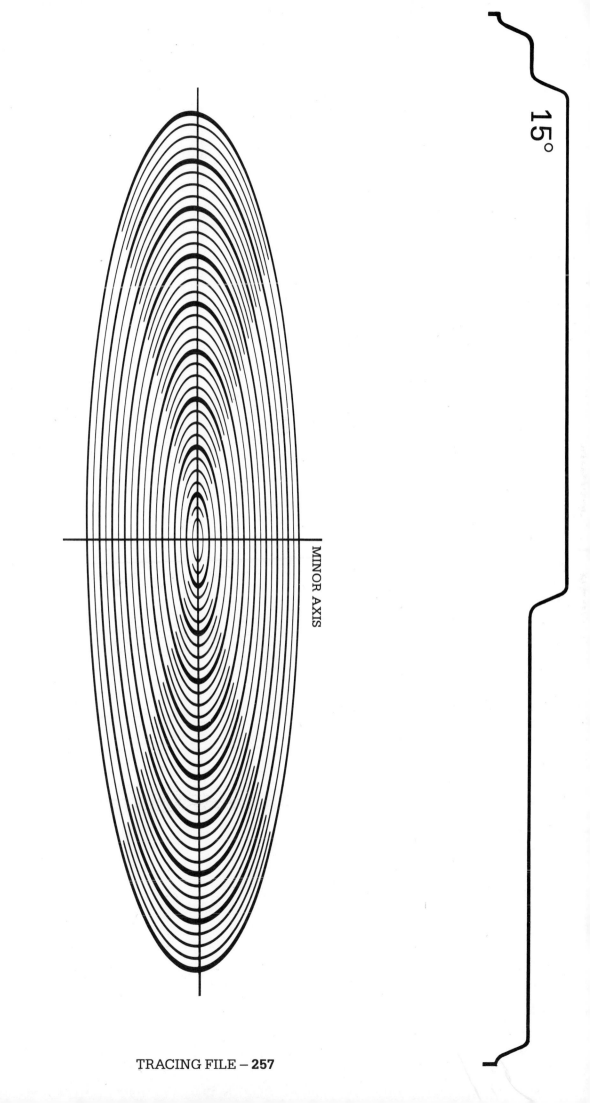

MINOR AXIS

15°

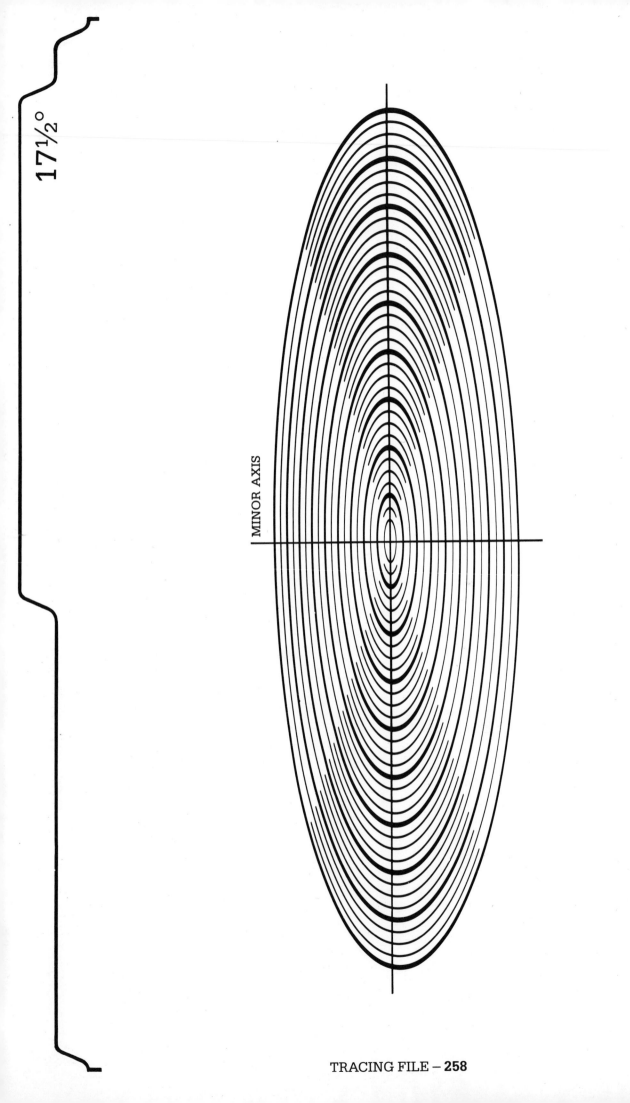

17½°

MINOR AXIS

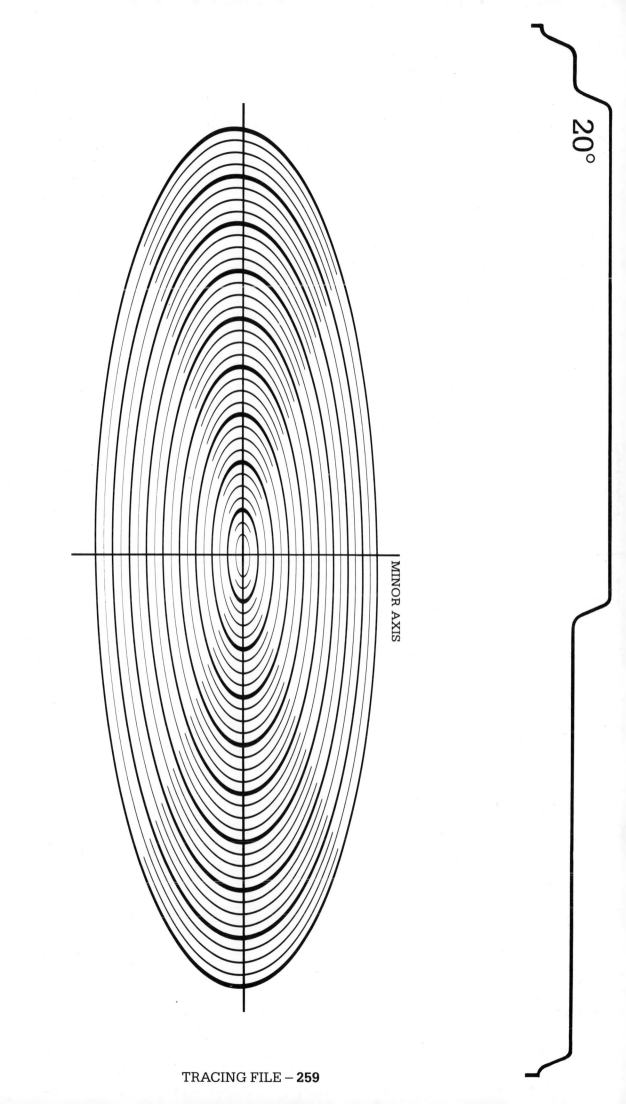

20°

MINOR AXIS

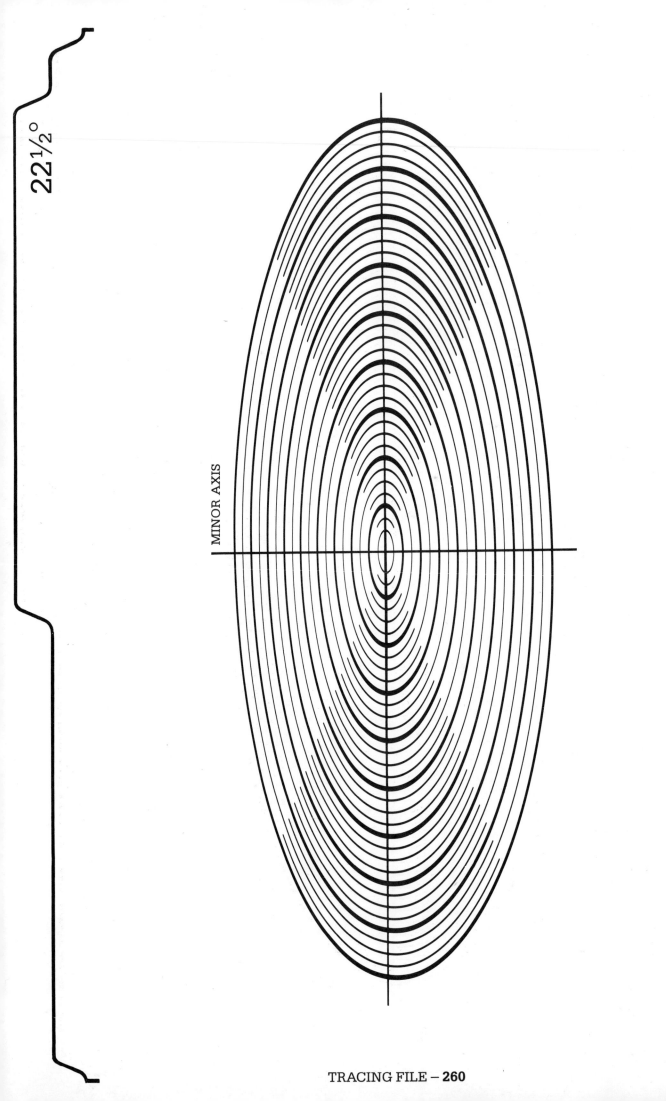

22½°

MINOR AXIS

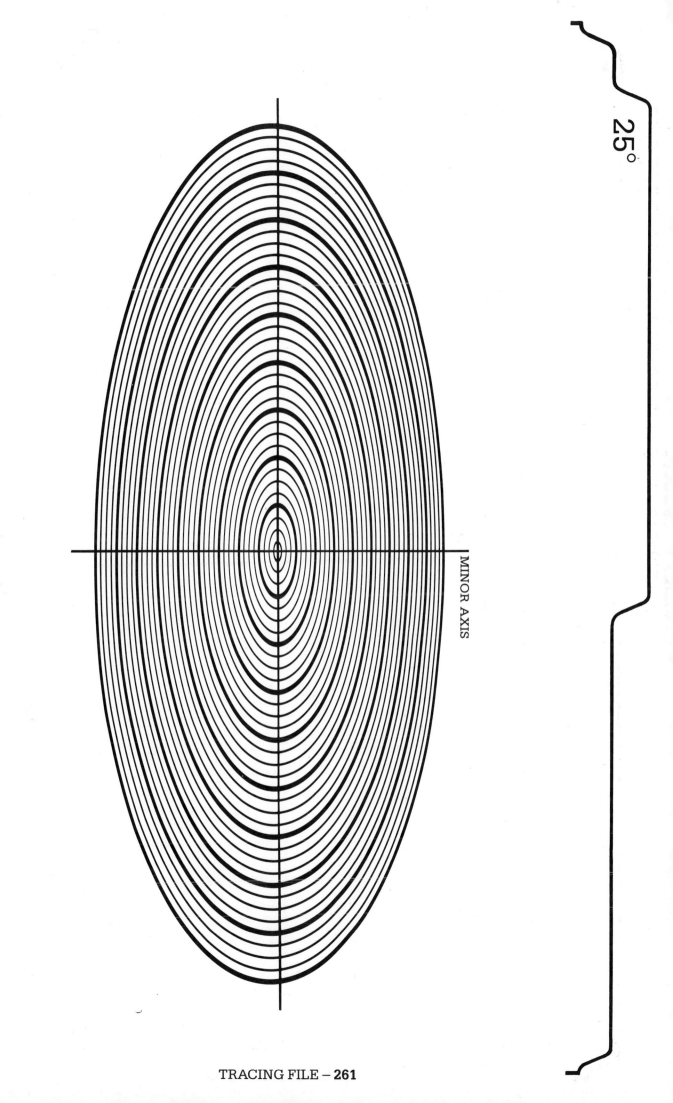

25°

MINOR AXIS

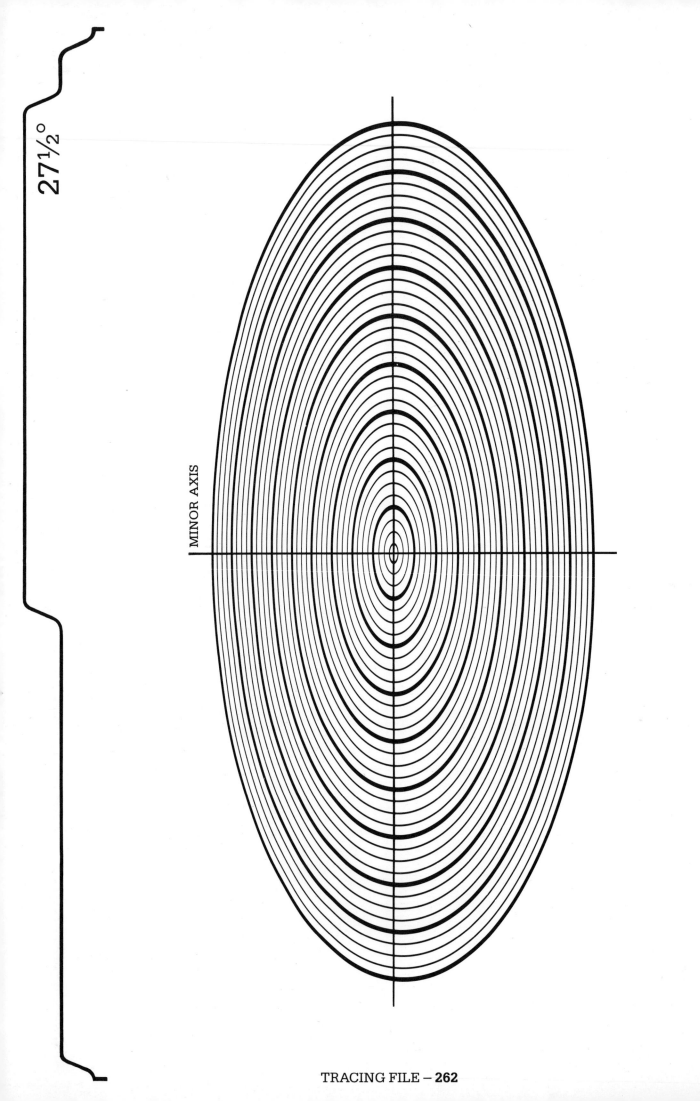

27½°

MINOR AXIS

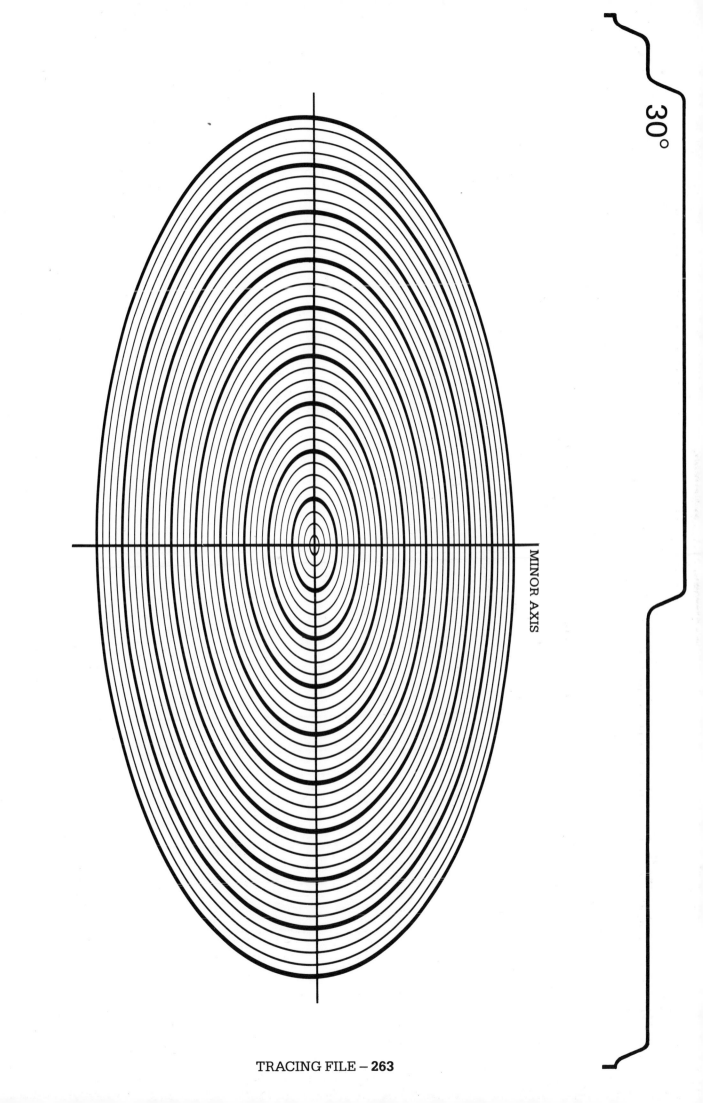

MINOR AXIS

30°

32½°

MINOR AXIS

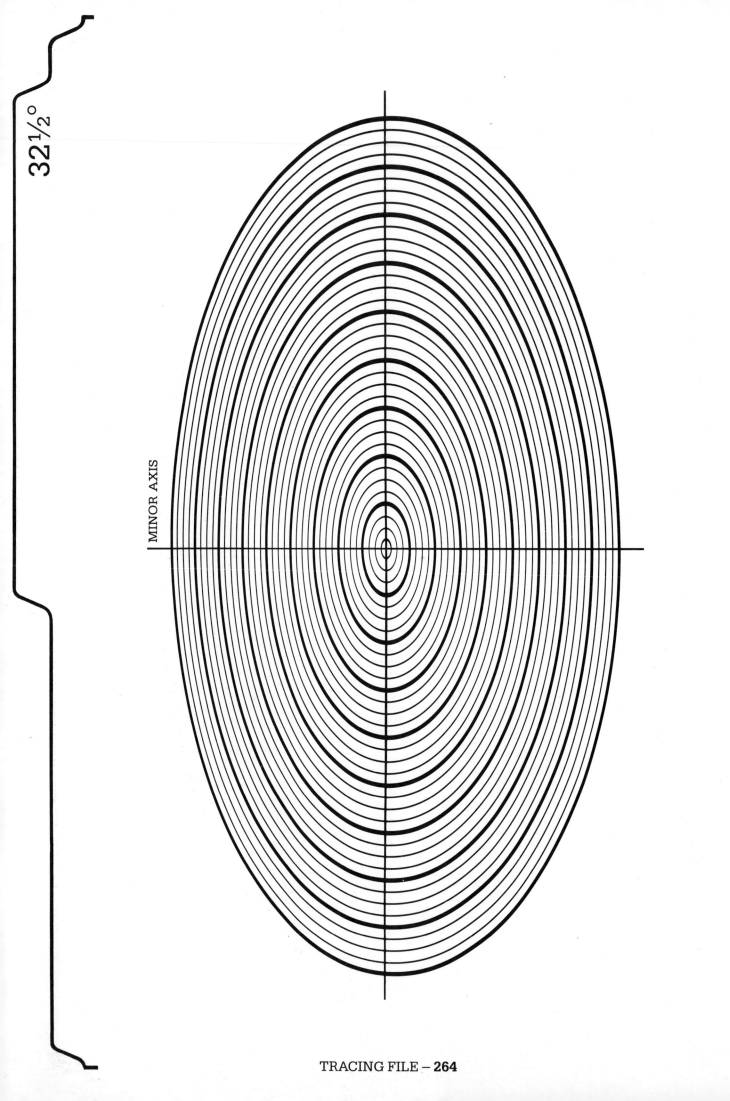

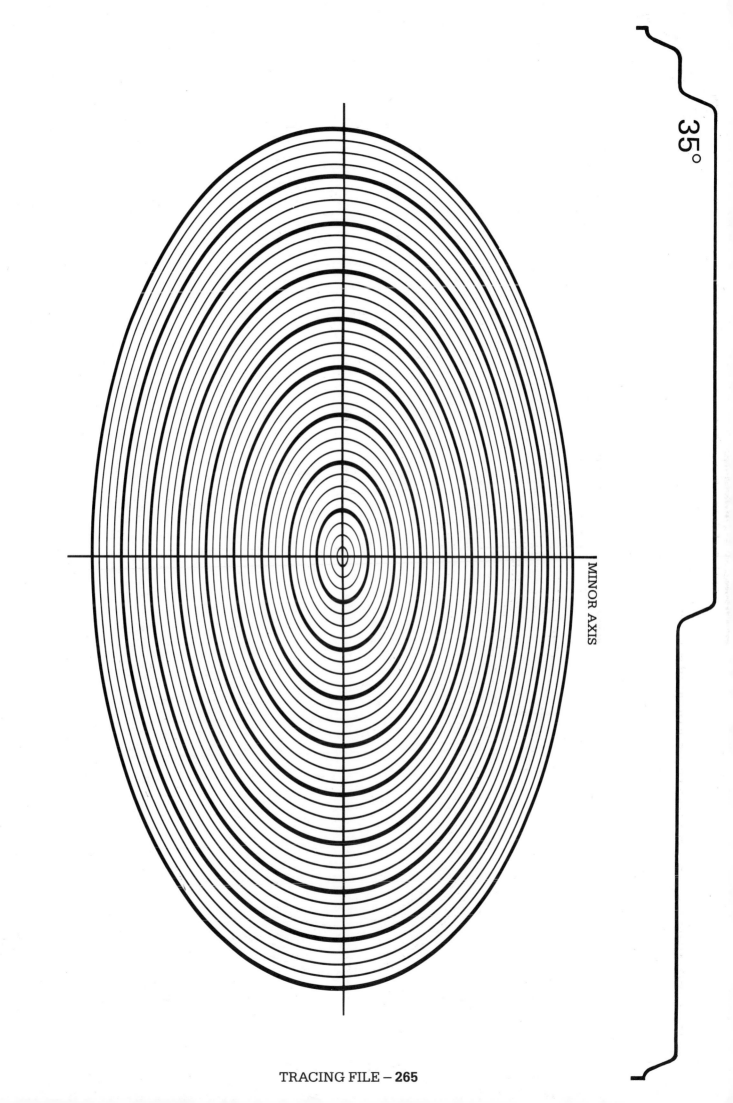

35°

MINOR AXIS

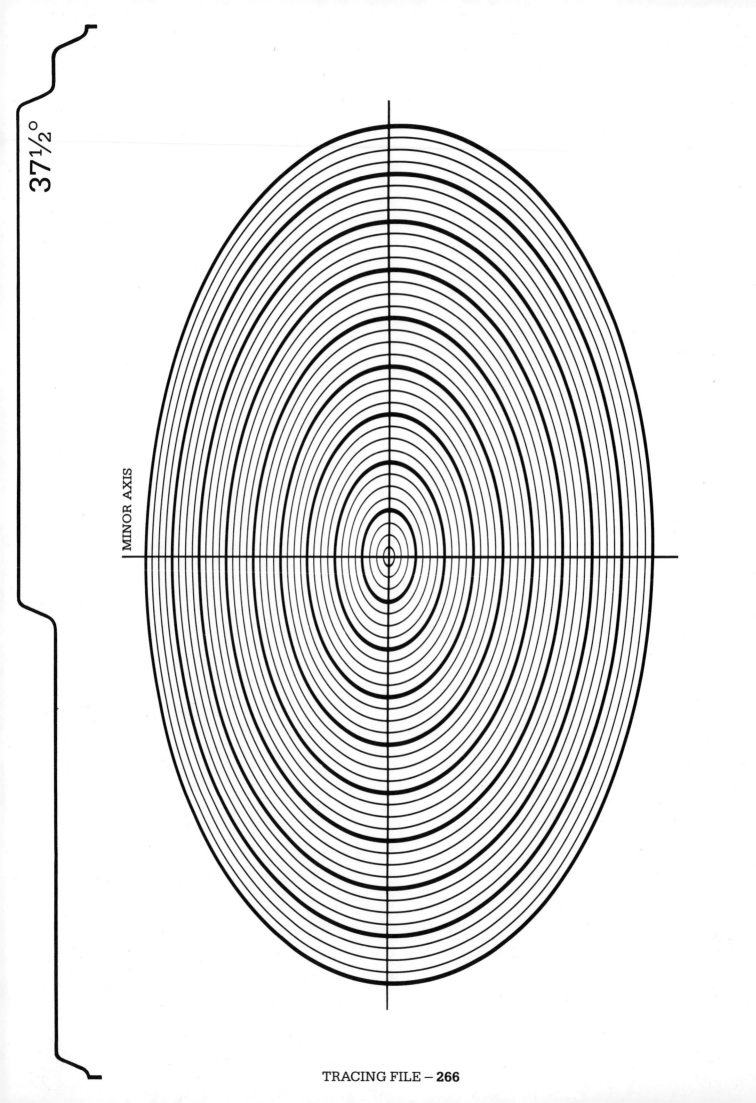

$37\frac{1}{2}°$

MINOR AXIS

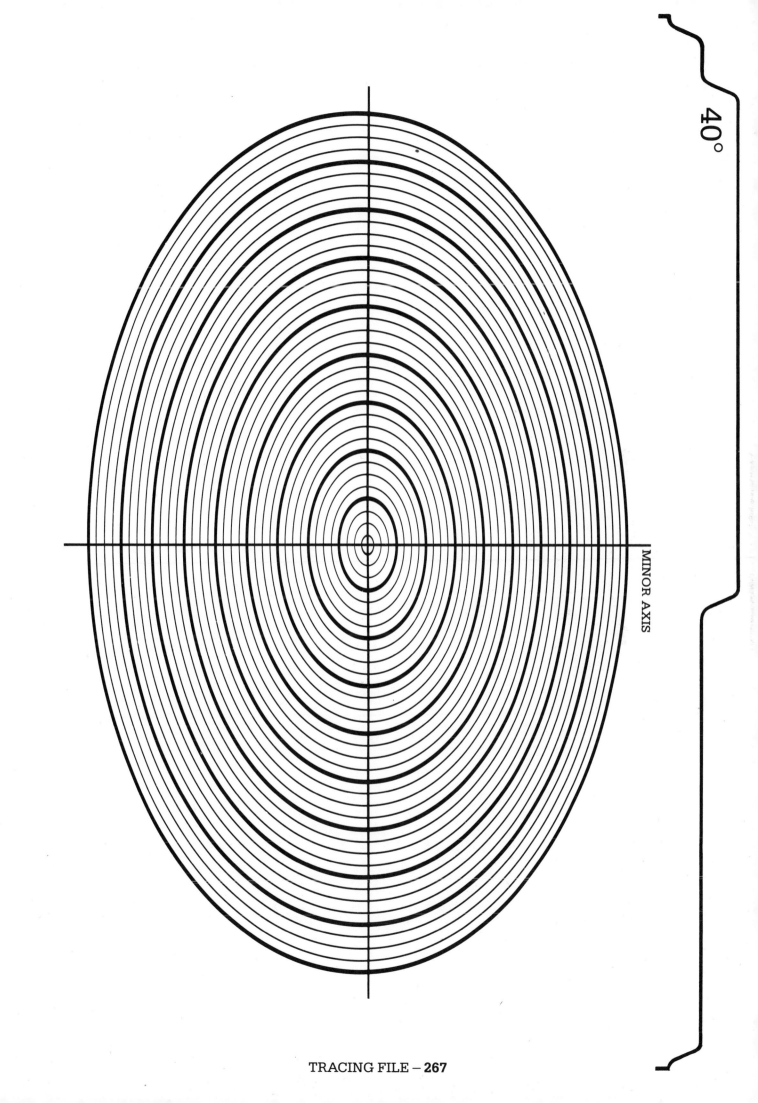

40°

MINOR AXIS

42½°

MINOR AXIS

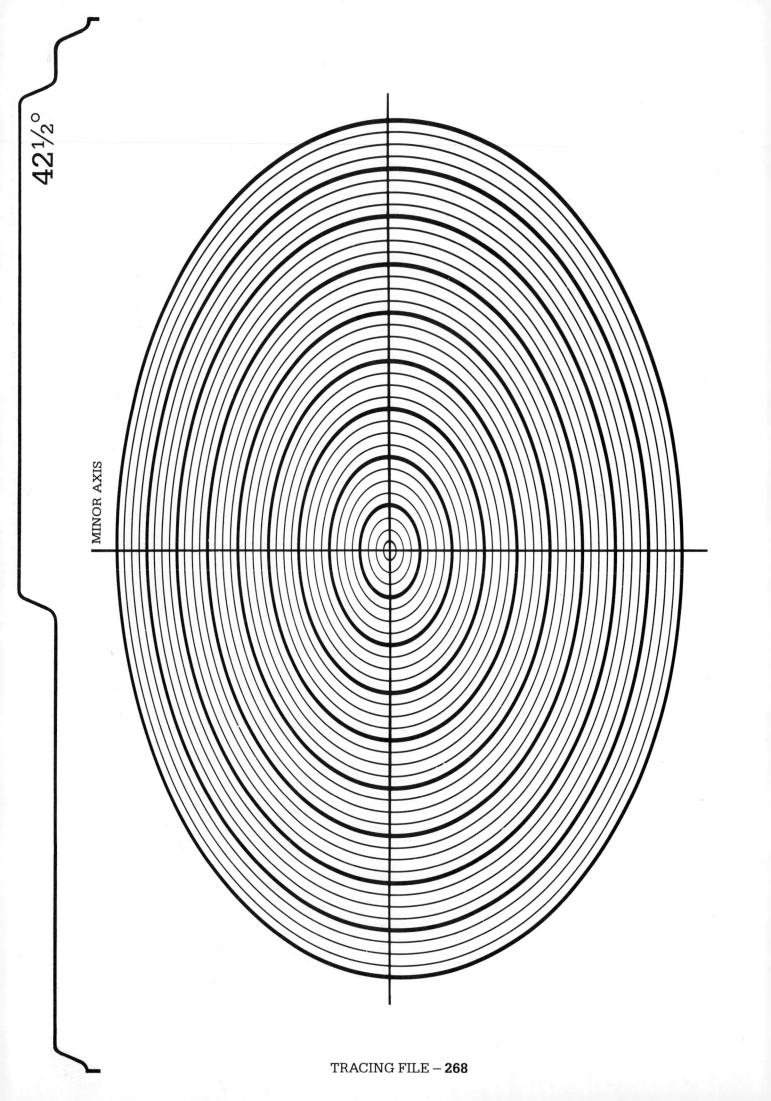

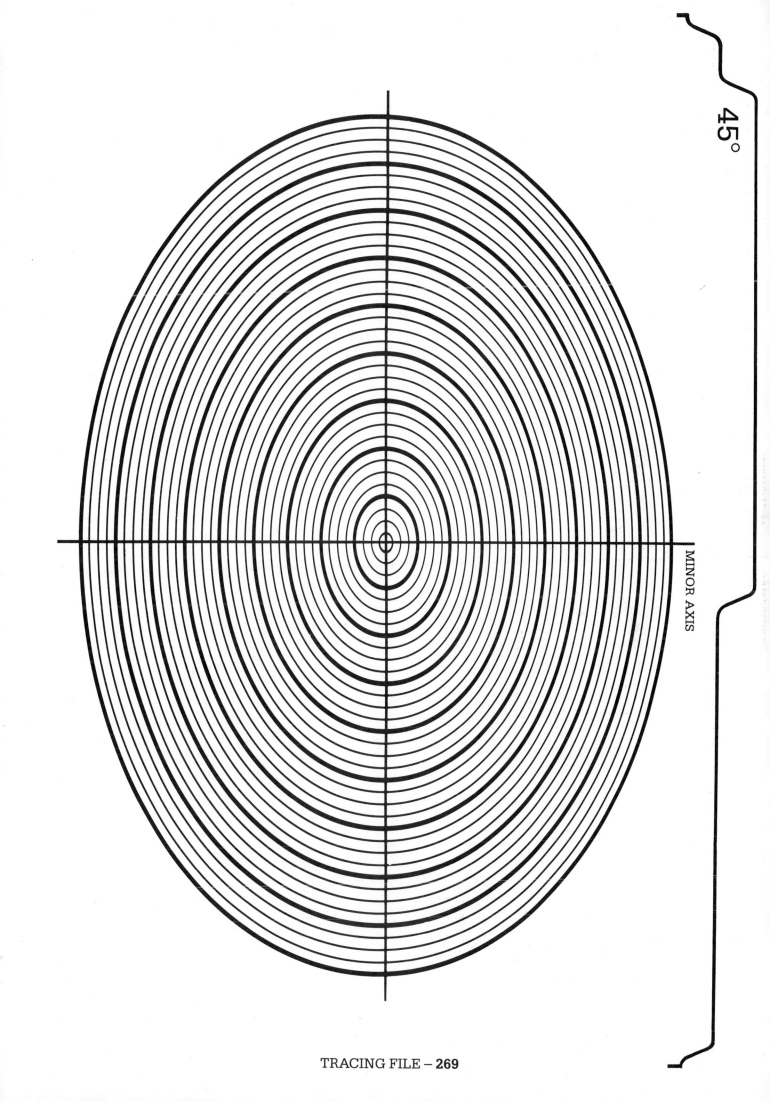

45°

MINOR AXIS

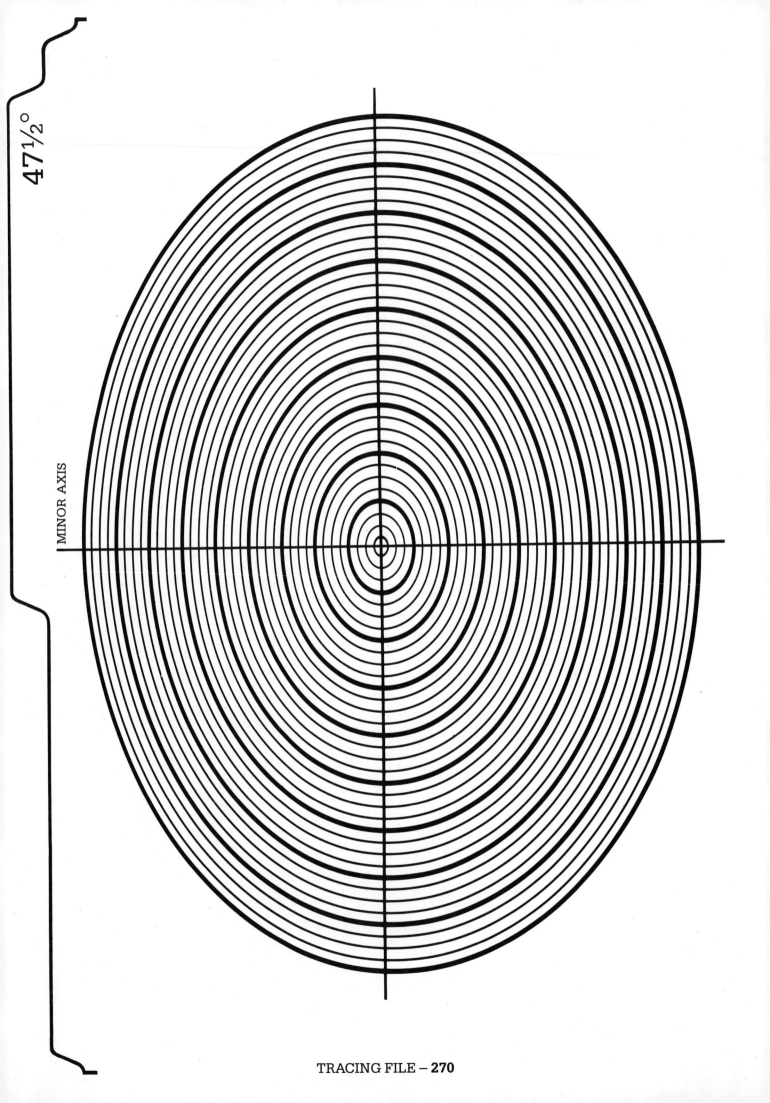

47½°

MINOR AXIS

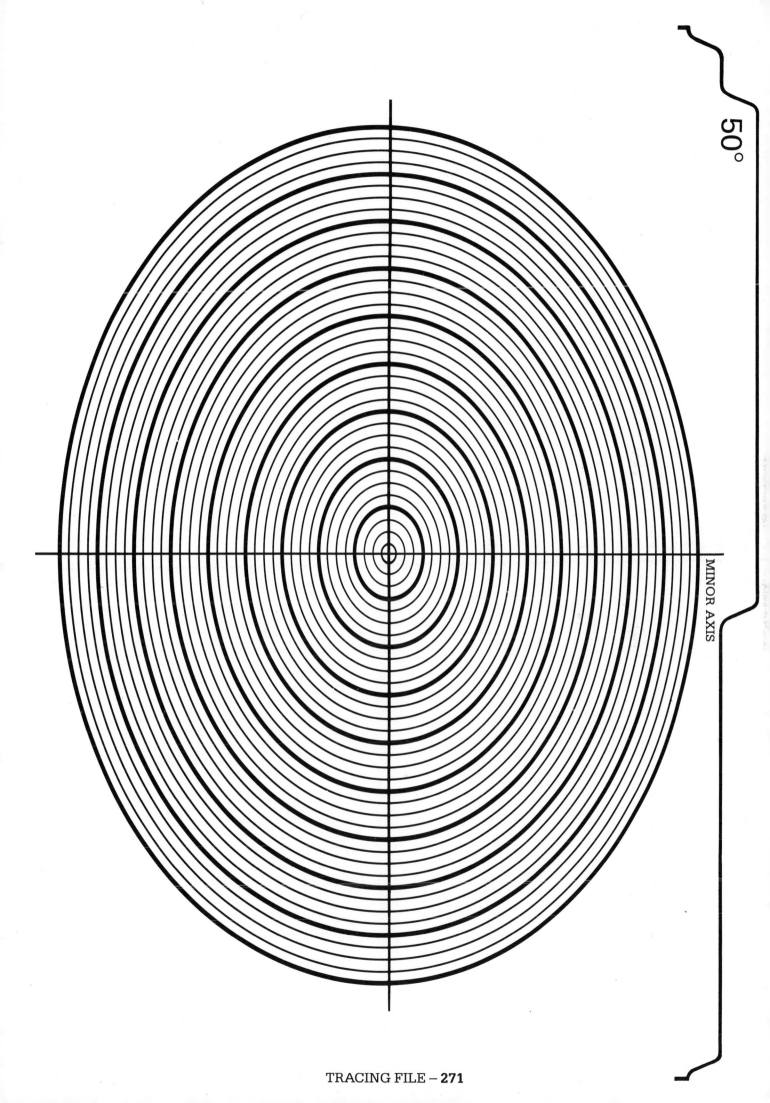

50°

MINOR AXIS

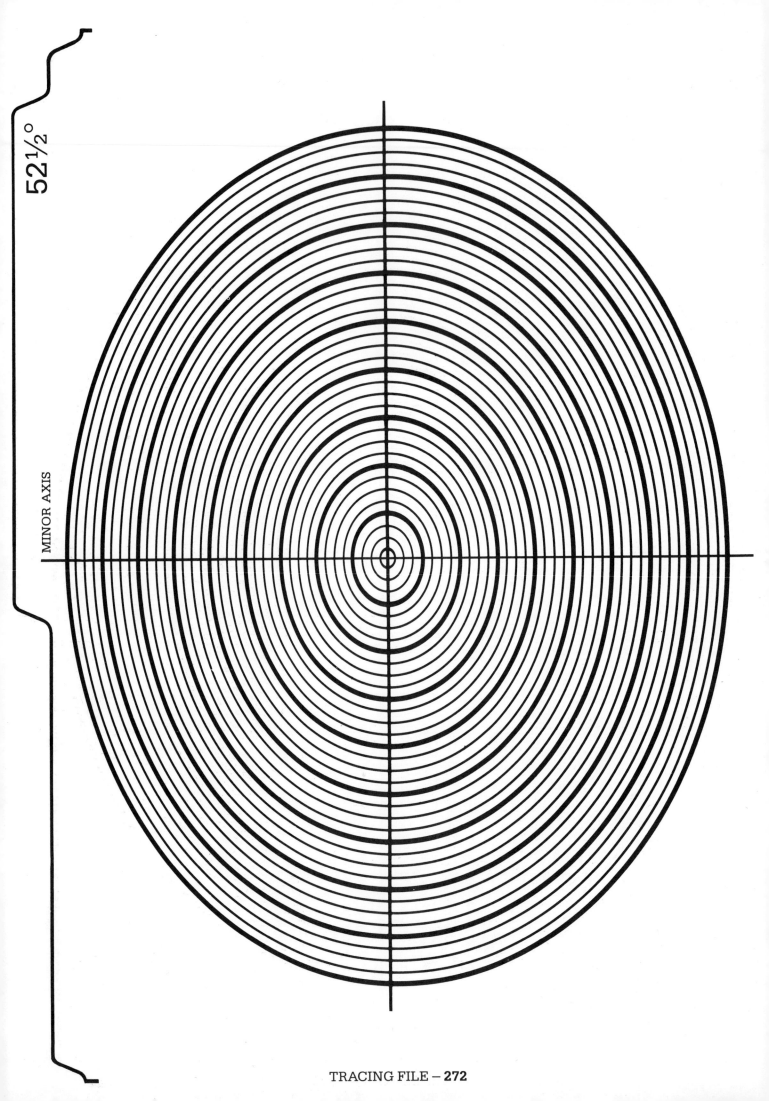

52½°

MINOR AXIS

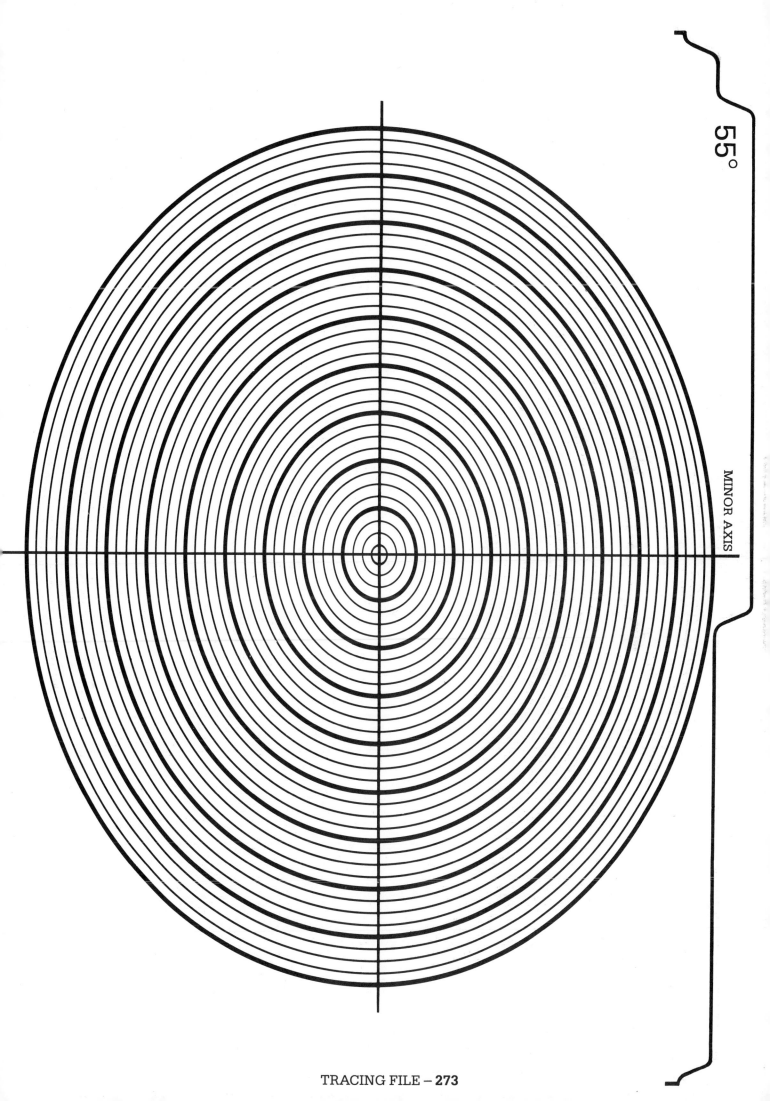

55°

MINOR AXIS

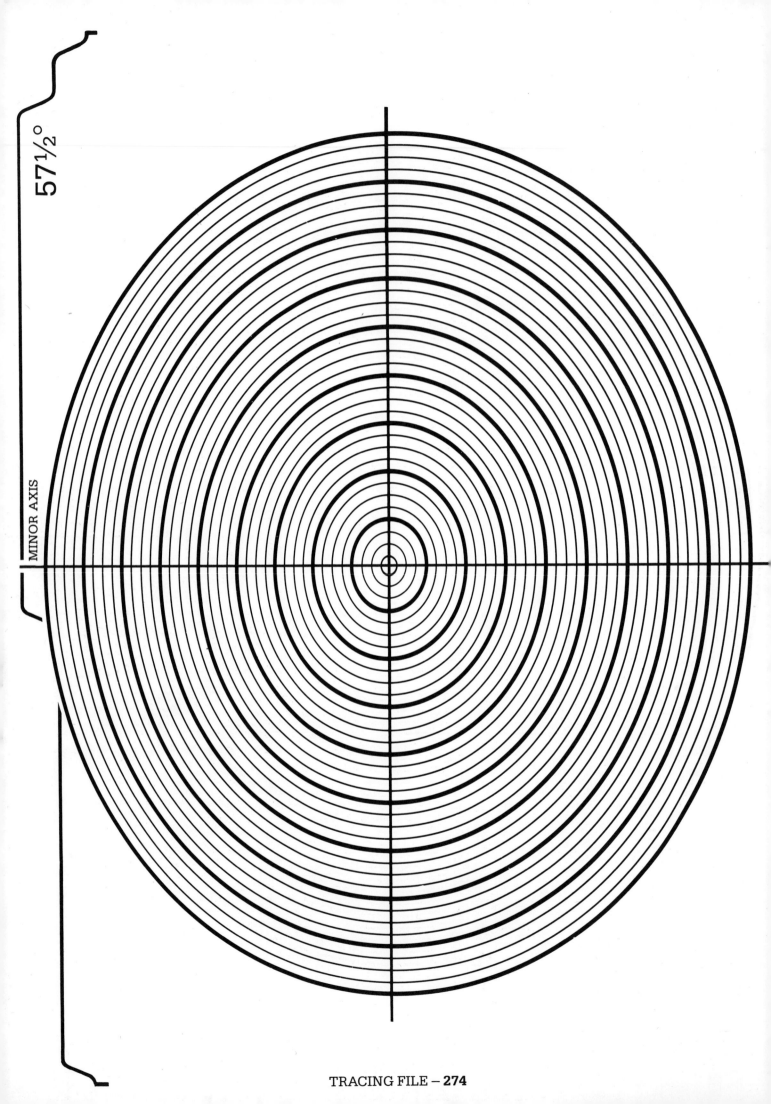

57½°

MINOR AXIS

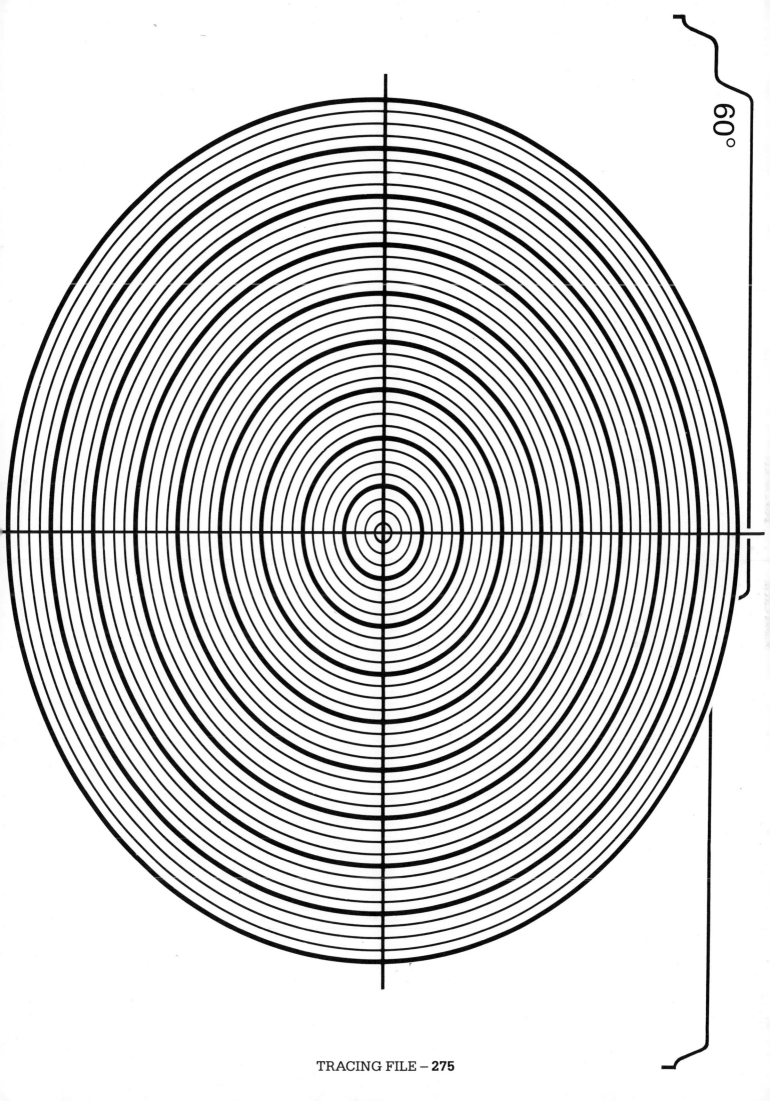

60°

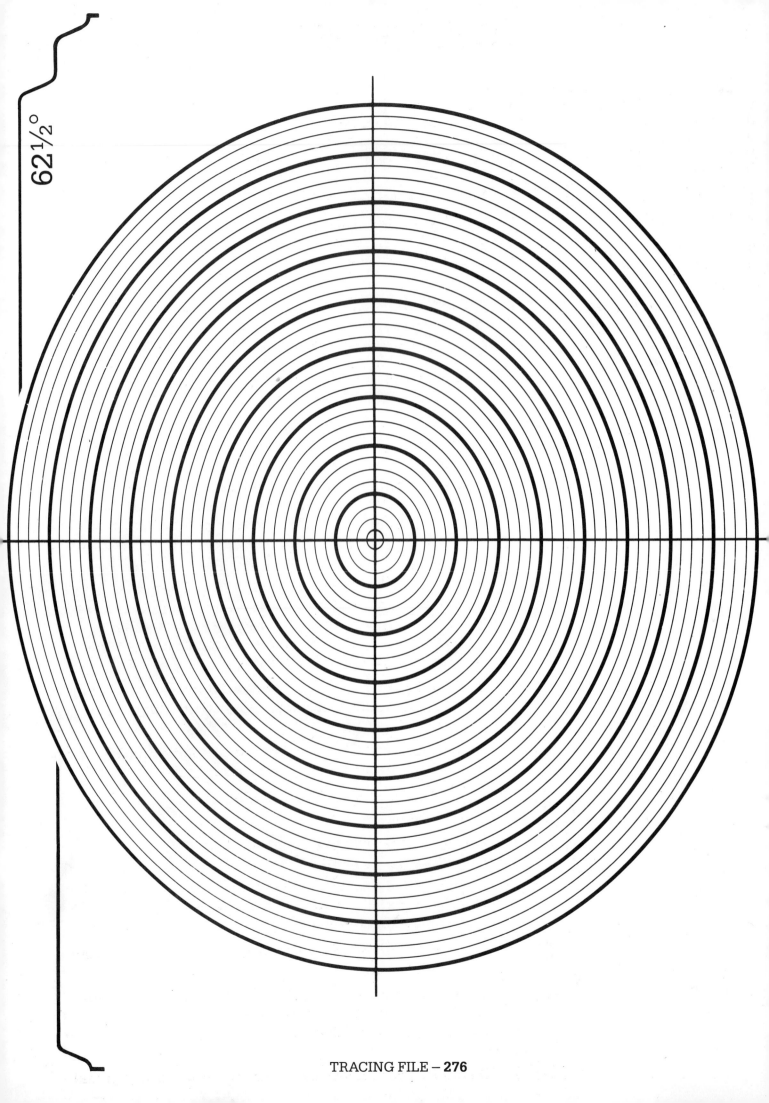

62 1/2°

CHECKLIST

Many designers believe the art of architectural rendering to be the exclusive domain of the artistically talented and consider a handsome rendering as a brilliantly executed inspiration. But this is all wrong. Excellence in rendering is not reserved for the inordinately talented. A superior architectural or interior illustration is not so much the result of artistic genius as good, basic drawing skills, a clear understanding of the purpose of the picture, and attention to detail.

The following notes focus on these qualities. They are designed to be used as a checklist while developing a rendering and as a tool to critique your finished picture.

 Evaluate whom the rendering is addressed to and what its purpose is—such as owner/preliminary design approval, zoning board/variance request, lender/financing approval, prospective buyer/sales display. Each situation requires a slightly different approach. If your picture could talk to your prospective audience, what do you want it to say?

 Try to capture the spirit or feeling of the design. A rendering should be animated and fascinating, not simply factual—working drawings serve that purpose.

 Give the picture a clear focal point and use compositional elements to lead the eye to it. Have cast shadows and key human figures directed toward the focal point where possible, and position strong vertical shapes at the edge of the picture to contain eye movement within the picture.

 Use overlapping of objects within the rendering to enhance the feeling of depth. See how many layers of objects you can develop between the foreground and background. Don't hesitate to cover up part of a picture element so long as no important visual information is lost.

 Draw and paint with clear, self-assured strokes. Bold, crisp work—even if slightly inaccurate—looks better than timid accuracy.

 Simplify. Eliminate or downplay distracting details that do not contribute to the purpose of your picture.

 Highlight important points with high contrast, sharp detail, and strong color.

 Use entourage elements to soften architecture and enliven repetitive areas of a picture.

 People used in a composition should "tell a story" about the design. They ought to be posed and appropriately dressed to describe and enhance their environment.

 Develop strong contrasts of light and dark. Avoid excessive use of middle values.

 Use counterpoint (the weaving of related but independent melodies throughout a composition) in art as in music. Let the interplay of several different visual themes sweep across your picture.

 Glamorize your subject. Sell the sizzle as well as the steak!

ABOUT THE AUTHOR

Richard M. McGarry graduated with honors from Miami-Dade Community College, and continued his professional education at the University of Florida and the Art Center College of Design before opening his own architectural and interior illustration office in 1975 in Miami, Florida. His firm, Richard M. McGarry Inc., has created presentation renderings for a wide range of design projects, including hotel and restaurant interiors, historic restoration ventures, cruise ships, office towers, hospitals, shopping malls, and housing developments.

INDEX

73 518MI 6764
11/01 30025-6 NULE